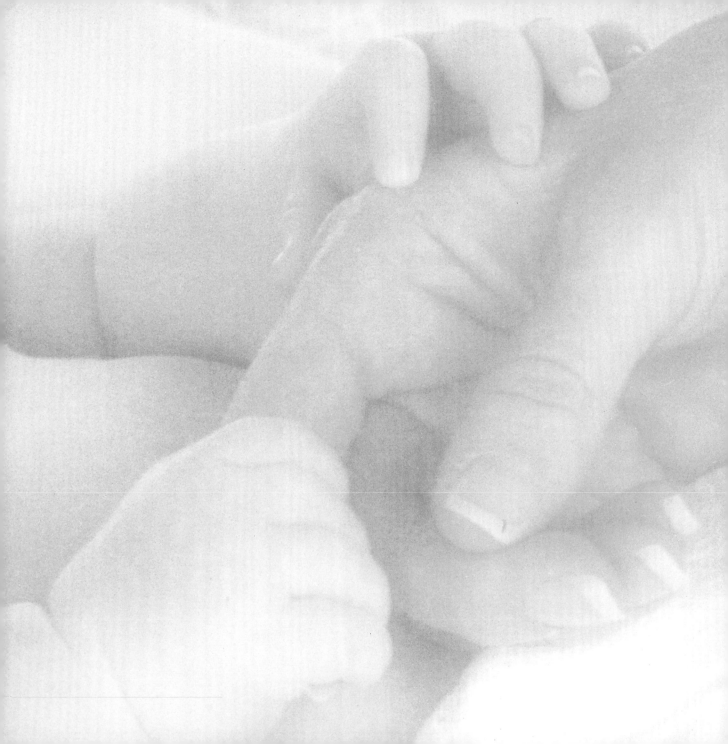

આ

At every child's birth,

a mother is born.

ᴥ

My child, in you I see me.

My mirrored self is reflected in your effervescent laughter, funny little stride,

even the tilt of your head. I marvel when you carry a tune,

skate smoothly as a swan, or curl up in bed with a good book.

Some things I wish I didn't see—stubbornness, impatience, fretting about the unknown.

How could I have kept you from "borrowing" these things from me?

—*Marjorie Lee Chandler, Solvang, California*

🙎

God gives us

beautiful gifts.

For me, one

is being a mother.

—*Susan Petrovits, Kodiak, Alaska*

🙎

"Bye, I love you," my children shout to me as they leave for school in the mornings.

It warms my heart to know that my kids are not ashamed to tell the world that they love me. May it always be so.

—*Linda Crawford, San Diego, California*

🙎

I watch you play, learn, and grow.

I am thankful that I am not enough for you anymore.

While it saddens me that you are growing away from me,

I hope that I will always be your friend, as well as your mom.

—*Phyllis Meyers, Albuquerque, New Mexico*

Sick on the couch
eyes closed against the world,
I feel my mother's touch
gently stroking my cheek
touching my hair.
Saying without words
"Where does it hurt?"
"I love you."
My mother
many miles away
could not be here.
I open my eyes.
My daughter
kisses my forehead.
She has inherited
my mother's touch.

—*Deborah Potter Wilkins, Wildwood, Missouri*

I am watching as my oldest child is getting ready for her first day of kindergarten, and I see the first of so many steps.

I want to hold her back and keep her little for just a while longer, but I know I cannot tie her down.

For tomorrow she will be that young college grad off to conquer the world. I just pray that I am ready when she is.

—*Vicki Aardema, Alexandria, Virginia*

Photo/Bachmann, Falls Church, Virginia

A MOTHER'S TOUCH

The Difference a Mom Makes

with an Introduction by Elisa Morgan

TEHABI BOOKS

TEHABI BOOKS

Tehabi Books developed and produced *A Mother's Touch*
and has conceived and produced many award-winning
books that are recognized for their strong literary
and visual content. Tehabi works with national and
international publishers, corporations, institutions, and
nonprofit groups to identify, develop, and implement
comprehensive publishing programs. Tehabi Books is
located in San Diego, California.
www.tehabi.com

MOPS International, Inc.
P.O. Box 102200, Denver, CO 80250-2200
www.mops.org

Elisa Morgan   *Senior Editor*
Carol Kuykendall   *Editor*
Mary Beth Lagerborg   *Managing Editor*

President and Publisher: **Chris Capen**
Senior Vice President: **Tom Lewis**
Vice President, Development: **Andy Lewis**
Editorial Director: **Nancy Cash**
Director, Sales and Marketing: **Tim Connolly**
Director, Trade Relations: **Marty Remmell**
Director, Corporate Publishing and Promotions: **Eric Pinkham**
Project Coordinator: **Mo Latimer**
Editor: **Sarah Morgans**
Manuscript Editor: **Laura Georgakakos**
Copy Proofer: **Kathi George**

Library of Congress Cataloging-in-Publication Data
has been applied for.

ISBN 1-887656-82-0

Contents

"*A Mother'*

I have to admit, parts of me were unsure I really wanted to be a mother, even though I waited and waited for four and a half years to adopt my daughter and then another hunk of time for my son. There were cloudy nights when I paced the floor and wondered, *Do I have what it takes to be a mom? Will I really make a difference in the life of this little one or could just anybody be the mom?* Fears of inadequacy and doubts tripped me at each developmental step my children took.

That I, who consider myself a Mother Inferior, have ended up the head of a mothering organization is a supreme irony. Me? With my doubts and struggles? Yep. Me. Over the past years of nurturing other mothers, I've learned an important lesson for moms like me everywhere: I am the mother my children need, and my touch in their lives today will shape them forever.

Mothers make an incredible difference in our world. When a mom wrestles her body from sleep to get up, yet again, with a fussy six-month-old, she touches that child's life today for tomorrow. When a mother ties shoe after shoe, and then folds her hands and watches chubby fingers attempt the process, her patience makes a difference in that child's life. When a mother invests the effort to discipline her wandering teen, her return can only be measured over the long haul. When a mother loves enough to embrace and then step back from her almost-adult child, her touch enables that child to step out and become an adult. And when a mother accepts assistance from an adult child—help in and out of bed, aid to and from the store, taxiing back and forth from the doctor's office—even in this stage, the mother's touch makes a difference in the life of her child.

At MOPS (Mothers of Preschoolers) International we focus on moms in the beginning stages of their mothering roles. We believe that when a child is born or adopted, a mother is born as well. As we celebrate our twenty-fifth year encouraging mothers and affirming women who choose to make a difference through their mothering, we have created *A Mother's Touch: The Difference a Mom Makes* as our way of commending all moms for the crucial role they play in our society.

This book includes moving tributes and candid images that convey the impact mothers have on the lives of their sons and daughters. But what I love best about *A Mother's Touch* are the voices of the mothers themselves. Here are thoughts rarely expressed but deep enough to have made a difference, not only in the lives of their children, but in the life of the mother herself. To me, what is best conveyed through these pictures and reflections is the immense courage and strength it really takes to be a mom. Despite the obvious demands of motherhood, these moms seem to express an underlying sense of quiet joy and privilege as women who have responded to the call. Many of these mothers express thoughts I myself have had. Indeed, we who are moms do belong to a remarkable society in which membership is determined less by the actual birth of a child and more by our own birth into motherhood.

I invite you to turn each page that follows and celebrate with us the difference made by a mother's touch through this photographic and literary tribute.

—*Elisa Morgan, President and CEO, MOPS International*

Louis DeLuca, Dallas, Texas

I once read an article
that said a mother lion only
roars when her cubs
are in danger.
These days I think of
that mother lion,
of how I am like her.
Most of the time I try to
remain calm as I
raise my four children
but every now and again
a fierce roar rumbles
from within me.

—*Ann Marie Drop, Iowa City, Iowa*

April Saul/Philadelphia Inquirer, Philadelphia, Pennsylvania

Oh, how I love to hold my little ones close especially when they're sad, touching their hair or faces, rocking them back and forth.

Isn't it amazing how no one ever has to teach a mother how to comfort her own child?

—*Katy McCleskey, Indianapolis, Indiana*

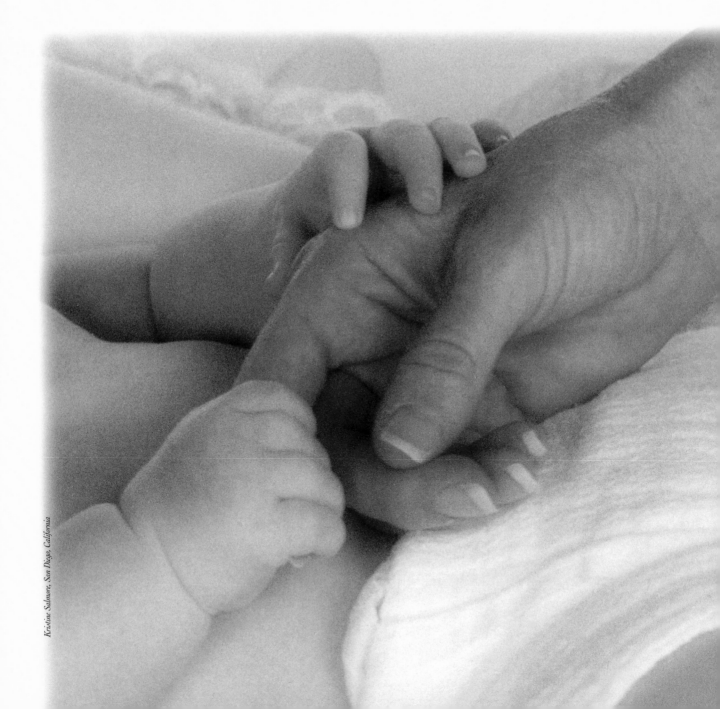

Finally, at 7:00 A.M. I watched my first grand-child's head crowning. One last intense push, and with a rush of water and blood, Christopher was in the world. In moments he was wailing in my arms. I could barely see him through the water of all grandmothers coming out of my eyes. So many births in that room; my son, Steven, a newborn father. Kathy, a newborn mother. I, a newborn grandmother. Our lives changed forever because of newborn Christopher. I know every birth, however ordinary, is extraordinary. Against my old breast I held the holy once again.

—*Barbra Minar, Solvang, California*

Louis DeLuca, Dallas, Texas

I never imagined the beauty of motherhood until you arrived. The way you get lost in my eyes sharing those love-filled moments when you smile at me, curl up to me, cry for me; watching you sleeping, being there when you awaken. I'm so thankful to God for having every day with you.

—*Rosa Nichols, Poway, California*

I was spellbound at becoming a mother. How could God trust me so?

—*Barbara Gordon, Chappaqua, New York*

❧

Has your heart

ever exploded at

Seeing a smile

Comforting a sadness

Feeling the softness

Soothing the tears

Cherishing the hugs

Loving the whole

Tasting the hurt

Hearing the love

Reading the eyes

of a child?

—*Rhonda L. Schultz,*

Hobart, Indiana

❧

It makes me feel so complete to look at my child's

angelic face. Here is a small life that my husband

and I created.

—*Janine Zinn, Middletown, New York*

❧

I was there when they woke, played, ate, cried,

laughed, needed clean diapers, and went to sleep.

I kissed them just for pure joy.

—*Juanita Tamayo Lott, Silver Spring, Maryland*

Mark Richards, Mill Valley, California

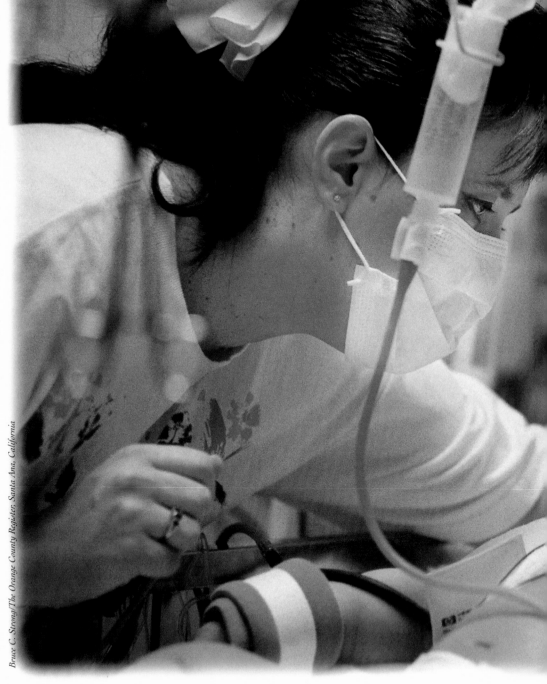

Nothing forces you to
live in the present
like raising a child.
—*Sharon Hershenhorn,*
Seattle, Washington

Oh, my little one,
I'd give my life
for you.
—*Rebecca Stephens,*
Conifer, Colorado

Bruce C. Strong/The Orange County Register, Santa Ana, California

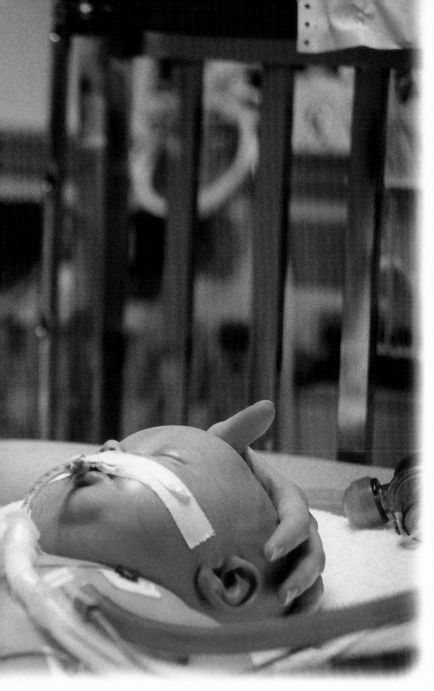

I never thought

I could love you so much

or hurt so badly

for another person.

It's impossible to tell you

just how much you

mean to me. . . .

You are my most precious

little girl.

Never forget that,

my Most Beautiful Angel.

Jennifer Girard, Hillsboro, Oregon

Al Cook, Lanexa, Virginia

You are my miracle baby,
Nicole. You were so anxious
to get here you appeared after
only twenty-six weeks.
You were so tiny, weighing
only one pound and six ounces,
but you were full of life and
love. The first time I saw you
and touched you I realized how
God truly works miracles.

—*Lidia Gonka, San Diego, California*

When was the magical day, the
one when I became a mother?
I'm not sure if it was the day
my son was born, or the first
time he said that enchanted
word, *Mommy*. I think the
reason I can't remember the
specific moment I became a
mother is because it's impossible
to imagine not being one.

—*Diana Cash, Sacramento, California*

So many people I meet

don't consider a stepmother

a "real mom."

But I ask myself whether

being a real mom is based

on biology and genetics

or rather on being a strong

and loving woman

who can guide

and encourage a child

as easily as being able

to comfort them

when they are hurt or scared.

A real mom has unconditional love

in her heart that is given freely

and that is who I am.

—*Michelle Tomm, Marlboro, Massachusetts*

Gus Chan, Cleveland Heights, Ohio

My husband says that I was born to be a grandmother.

Maybe so. I always knew I was born to be a mother.

My earliest childhood memories are of how moved

and protective I was in the company of smaller children.

After having six children, little did I expect

still another ocean of happiness waiting for me—grandchildren.

When they came, it was as if a wave of tenderness was drowning me,

a never-ending pool of generosity, of pleasure, and of wonder.

—*Lucrezia Ocampo Weidmer, Hallsville, Texas*

God miraculously sends the right child to the right mother. Nick and I like to count through all his cousins and friends

and marvel that they all ended up with just the right mothers . . . and how glad he is to have ended up with me!

—*Miriam Brownlee, Philadelphia, Pennsylvania*

Nita Winter, Sausalito, California

Moms as a rule are not really prepared

to face the realities of marriage and motherhood.

I was no exception. I practiced on my firstborn

and before I could get the hang of it,

along came the twins!

My passage from womanhood to motherhood

was and still is a learning process.

—*Ernesta Cooke, Oxnard, California*

Heidi Bratton, Salem, New Hampshire

❧

Breeze so thick

with dandelion stars

I stick out my tongue

to catch one,

like a snowflake.

I watch the children

run together

on the grassy hill,

a school of fish

weaving in unison.

Someday you will be

one of them,

but now I blink back

my disbelief

and cherish my secret.

I am pregnant with you.

—Eva McGinnis, Federal Way, Washington

❧

While expecting, I was always told my life would be so different, but no one ever said how much better it would be.

—Tonya Roberts, Bardstown, Kentucky

"I Love You"

2 4

When I was a child, my mother's lap was the warmest and safest place in the world. On my mother's lap, all the troubles of childhood would fade away, and I would be perfectly secure and content.

I remember simply sitting on her lap for long periods of time. I suspect she had dishes to do, clothes to wash, errands to run, and yet, I sat. But I do not recall her ever telling me she had something to tend to. In fact, it was always I who ventured off first. Perhaps I had finally awakened from sleep, or my childhood hurts had been comforted away, but when I was emotionally full, I got up.

My mother had two children younger than I, so how was she able to provide this precious gift of time? I wondered this yesterday, when my own two-year-old daughter, still drowsy from nap time, curled up on my lap. I stroked her hair softly, sang sweet lullabies, and eventually, when she was ready to face the world, she got up.

So Much"

My memories of childhood tugged at my heart. Only then did I realize how my own mother managed that special lap time. She had allowed chores to wait.

My mother had given me two precious gifts, one to her daughter the child, the other to her daughter the adult. To the child, she gave comfort, love, security, and intimacy. To the adult, she modeled a valuable lesson: that a mother's lap is a child's sanctuary. Thanks, Mom; I needed both.

—*Carla Risener Bresnahan*

Karim Samat-Basha, Birmingham, Alabama

Tom Watson, Skaneateles Lake, New York

❧

It was time to take the baby home. As a nurse watched the
two of us dress Casey for the trip home, I worried
that if we couldn't get his little stretch-suit on the
right limbs, we might be detained as unfit parents.

—*Marni Jackson, Toronto, Ontario*

❧

Raising a child—teaching, encouraging,
disciplining—through all this, does he know I love him?
This morning I received my answer.
My rambunctious toddler crawled into my lap
and, laying the sweetest of kisses on my cheek, said,
"Momma, you're my best friend."
My heart is still singing.

—*Dawn Lewis, Encinitas, California*

❧

When is a mother born? I think I was born a mother with the first echoes of my baby's heartbeat, which I heard just a few weeks ago.

Though not yet in my arms, my infant's heart calls to me, bringing out in me the need to love and protect, to cherish and encourage.

With each kick and roll, tuck and twirl, the life dancing inside me confirms what I have just discovered—

a mother is born the moment she feels the love in her heart for a child she has never seen.

—*Theresa Meyers, Phoenix, Arizona*

My little one, you hold my gaze deeply and without hesitation. The shared emotion of love that passes between us during that gaze

is one of the most profound revelations you've shared with me. Everyone told me that I would be amazed at how much I would love you.

But until we made eye contact, for the first time, and now for the uncountable millionth, I didn't realize how connected I am to you,

and to mothers everywhere and throughout all time. Thank you for sharing this secret with me, precious baby.

—Kristen Dillon Lummis, Grand Junction, Colorado

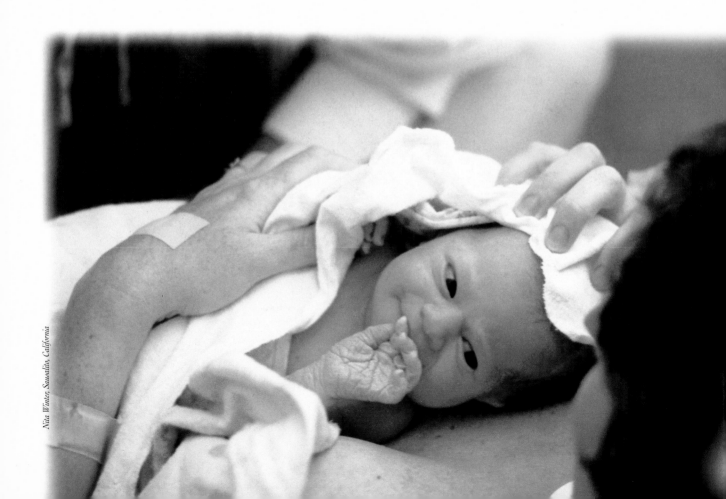

Nita Winter, Sausalito, California

I adopted my daughter, Katie, from China

when she was only nine months old

and I was forty-seven and single.

A case of middle-aged insanity? Not on your life!

The moment I held her in my arms

I knew Someone Really Big

had brought us together.

—*Ann Spangler, Tucson, Arizona*

Ethel Wolvovitz, Brooklyn, New York

No one could have prepared me for this.

Nothing I had read or seen could describe the exquisite joy of my soul. "I'm a mother!" Me! Oh, heart, be still.

Who is this sweet, pink face—so fresh from heaven—peeking out from beneath her blanket cocoon?

Oh, God, you have such faith and trust in me.

Please stay close and whisper in my ear the things I need to know. I want to do my best.

—*Kathy Erickson, Freedom, Wyoming*

Anthony, when you were five years old

I thought it best for you to live with your dad

so you would have a fatherly influence in your life.

I lived for the times you'd come to visit—

the holidays and summer vacations.

You were such a delight to me.

I hope you understand how difficult it was for me

to make this decision. Even though we were apart,

I thought of you every minute of every day.

—*Anita Hudson Speier, La Jolla, California*

NURTURER

John Korom, Wauwatosa, Wisconsin

How short a time since

I bore you in womb, in arms, in heart.

My labor pains return

Each time you plunge

Headfirst into the world, my child.

You've come to go

From my lap, my knee, my side

But never from my love.

Like Abraham with Isaac

I give you up—I receive you again.

Forever, my child.

—*Vicki Huffman, Nashville, Tennessee*

I realized after the first few days

that this was what I had been waiting for

and working toward all of my life.

Nothing else I had done,

or would ever do would be as important,

or perfect as having this child

and being this child's mother forever.

—*Janet Chambers, Davis, California*

Dorothy Littell Greco, Boston, Massachusetts

&

Kitchen Dancing

The time? Midnight.

My gown? A fuzzy robe.

The music? A quiet radio.

The lighting? Dim glow of the digital clock.

My partner? A little bald man (only three months old).

We swing and sway in each other's arms

as the night ticks by, oblivious to the rest of the world.

My restless partner melts into my chest

and we become one . . . again.

Tonight I dream of a night on the town.

Someday, my dreams will be of kitchen dancing.

—*Susan Rockwell, Grandville, Michigan*

Barbara Maynard, Encinitas, California

ও

You feel the love and warmth that I am giving you through my touch

while you nurse at my breast. . . .

For one year and nine months we've shared this special bond.

This ability to nourish you is a gift from God;

it empowers me as a woman.

—*Venessa Watt-St. Clair, Teaneck, New Jersey*

ও

I always thought I would have six children—all boys!

At least that's what I wanted. Instead, I couldn't have any children.

I thought it was too late for me. Then, when I remarried, I was suddenly the

proud mother of a beautiful nine-year-old daughter.

She was a child so loving, she made up for six.

—*Nancy Cash, San Diego, California*

Your beautiful baby, your very own daughter.

You gave her part of my name. When I looked

at that tiny girl, my first grandchild

my only granddaughter,

I felt such a sense of continuity, a special bond.

My own mother had passed away by that time

and I longed for her

to share this experience with us.

But I felt her presence, somehow,

as I looked at the two of you.

—*Sharon Lewis, Del Mar, California*

Heidi Bratton, Salem, New Hampshire

Dorothy Littell Greco, Boston, Massachusetts

Cuddled against me is my twenty-seven-month-old daughter, Joanna, sound asleep.

As I watch her peacefully resting by my side, I can't imagine how I'm going to love the new baby—due to

be born tomorrow—as much as I love my daughter tonight. Looking down at her soft brown curls,

I wonder why I've put her in this position. Although I should know better,

it seems in some ways like I'm betraying my firstborn.

Do other moms ever feel this way when they have their second child?

—*Lynn Munger, Rochester, Michigan*

Liza Diomin, San Diego, California

"It's Okay,

The Canadian winter of 1957 was very hard. Life in general was growing harder and harder by the month, but I felt it right that I should shoulder my load in life, since I had that previous spring been confirmed and had entered adulthood thereby. Oh, yes I took my new station very seriously.

To me adulthood meant you did your duty yourself, without complaint. Certain honors were accorded the adult; but certain obligations were required in return. The honors sounded like this: "You're free, young man." I myself could, for example, choose what time I went to bed. But the obligations sounded like this: "Young man, you're on your own."

I was alone.

Therefore, I bore my responsibility within the family. I was the oldest of seven by then. I saw to the welfare of my sisters and brothers. I made sure they went to bed. I hollered at them.

My mother said, "Who died and left you boss?"

I said, "Yeah, but —" like any debating adult. "Yeah, but they ought to be quiet. Yeah, but they need their sleep. Yeah, but I'm only doing what you do, Mom."

My mother was in trouble in those days. I was helping her.

Don't Cry"

But she said, "Why aren't you in bed?"

I said, "I'm grown now."

"Grown," she said. "My son is grown." She folded her arms and stood back to get a better look. "And can he reap the whirlwind too," she said, "this man of mine?"

My enigmatic mama. Well, but I knew what she meant: You're on your own, boy.

Yes. No argument. I was so much on my own that even my mother didn't know that I had chosen to help her, nor could she know the cost. I was protecting her. She and my father had begun to suffer the malice of certain bitter people. A scourge of gossip swept our city, truly wounding my parents since this nastiness was directed at them in particular. Well, and I had seen the hurt in their faces. Slashed by loud lies. Their solid work riddled by whispers. Gossip is a sort of guerrilla warfare: it hits and quickly disappears before there can be a genuine engagement. Liars hide. And my mother sometimes sobbed in secret. But I heard her. I knew. Therefore I had taken it upon myself to keep at least their household peaceful. Yes, I bossed the kids to goodness, to silence, and to bed, and then I withdrew myself to consider the trouble my parents endured.

Winter was very hard that year. I felt lonely in my adulthood. But I accepted that loneliness uncomplainingly, as the due of an adult.

So be it. I would live with it. Forever.

And then one night I couldn't sleep at all. I was sick. My stomach kept knotting in spasms, and by two in the morning I had dampened the sheets with sweat. There was a winter wind outside, whistling at the eaves with the sort of solitary note which made my corner of the bedroom dark and lonely indeed. Awake this way, I seemed to be alone in the universe.

Now, I expected absolutely nothing. It never occurred to me but that I would have to handle this misery alone. I was an adult. Free. On my own.

But I must have been groaning out loud.

Because suddenly the hall light came on outside my door. Then the door swung inward. And there stood my mother, dark in a diaphanous white gown. Calm, quiet, and utterly beautiful.

"Walt, what's the matter?"

I was stunned. This I had not expected. Her presence and her voice alone—the familiarity of a voice which I had thought I'd never hear that way again—made me start to cry.

But I was fourteen years old then.

"Wally?" she whispered.

"My stomach," I sobbed.

"Oh, Wally!"

My mother floated toward me then and sat on the edge of the mattress, which sank to her weight. She put a cool hand to my forehead. "Yes, fever," she said. How long since she had sat beside me so? How long since she had kissed the little Wally? Long.

In the dark, her hair a nimbus by the hall light, she whispered, "Pull your knees up to your tummy. It'll ease you."

How holy the homely remedies! I did, and I cried and cried—for none of this should have been. I truly never thought that I could be a child again. Oh, I thought I had lost all that.

But I had a mother, after all, and she came to me. I was exhausting myself by protecting her in those days, not she me—and yet she came to me. I was fully adult, independent, self-sufficient, a reaper of the whirlwind, acceptor of all the consequences; I had forfeited the tender mercy of a mama in the nighttime. Nevertheless, she came to comfort me—and like a baby I curled into the crook of her arm and wept.

—*Walter Wangerin, Jr.*

Jennifer George-Walker, San Diego, California

☙

Dear Diary: Tonight on TV, a two-year old died and I am sobbing uncontrollably. The mom is holding him for the last time.

I am a mess—thinking about my own precious daughter, Mirella, only days since her birth. I don't even want to write it down . . . please, please don't let anything ever happen to her.

I couldn't handle it. So, I am sitting here wiping my face, wishing that Peter were here to hold me instead of being on his business trip, when Mirella starts crying.

I go to her, and she's apparently crying for no reason. She has her bunny, her binky, and she's covered. I pick her up, and her hair is sticking out every which way. I giggle.

I hold her to my shoulder, and she quiets down but is still a little fussy. I hum "A Dream Is a Wish Your Heart Makes," and she puts her head on my shoulder, contented.

I sway back and forth, savoring the moment. I lay her back down, she does the "tuck and roll" with bunny, and I tuck her in.

I have the best daughter in the world. She must've known I needed a hug. I hope we always have this connection.

—*Karyn Huber, Guilford, Connecticut*

Jonathon A. Meyers, Albuquerque, New Mexico

Why is it I can never finish anything?
There are always noses to wipe, spills to mop up, tears to
dry. I know there will come a day when my house will be
clean, a time when I can walk from room to room without
tripping over toys, or hearing the endless
bickering between kids. But then, I'll probably miss it.

—*Mary Ann Mooney, Sparks, Nevada*

Bruce C. Strong, Orange, California

Watching you throw a temper tantrum reminds me of
myself as a child. I remember all the times my mother said,
"Your grandmother wished one like me on me."
Now I know it's my turn.

—*Susan Kranzel, San Diego, California*

Ron Nickel, Three Hills, Alberta

Tears of joy, tears of pain. My tears are gifts

only a mother would understand.

—*Christine Caruso-Corley, Fairfield, California*

This custody battle is tearing me apart.

After the door shut behind those men

taking my son away, I panicked.

Mama, I don't remember how the phone

got into my hand, or the number got

dialed correctly, but when your voice

came on the line I knew everything

was going to be all right.

—*Diana Varner, Newport News, Virginia*

My mother died when I was a little girl,

but I find that, in mothering my son, I

mother myself. In holding and rocking

him, I am held and rocked. I am daily

being given the chance to define for

myself what mothering means.

—*Laura Georgakakos, Mt. Kisco, New York*

Kevin Vandivier, Austin, Texas

I never realized how vulnerable I was as Mommy, the protector, until the day I turned the corner while driving to the grocery store, and the car door flew open throwing my tiny daughter, Charmaine, out. Terrified, I stopped the car, fearing the wheel might have hit her. Her face had scraped into the dirt and was bloody, but she was okay. Later when we were home, and I was crying, Charmaine looked at me and said,

"Mommy, don't cry, you didn't mean to do it."

—Beth Law, San Luis Obispo, California

Greg Schneider, Redlands, California

Heidi Bratton, Salem, New Hampshire

I am the mother of a prodigal son. He has rejected me, and he has rejected God.

But my comfort is that God shares my pain. And he has not rejected either one of us.

—Lynn Butts, Englewood, Colorado

My son, Dylan, just turned one this month. Ever since he was brand new I've comforted him by rubbing or lightly scratching his back. This week has been especially hard for me. But on a recent evening we were sitting on the floor, playing, and he was growing tired and we were kind of cuddling, when he went to get his blanket and bottle and came back over to where I sat on the floor. He laid his head on my shoulder and reached around and started scratching my back in the most loving way. When I think of it I almost cry.

—*Teri Burris, Tomball, Texas*

❧

Today I feel shocked and angry that the kids are so demanding. It seems like they are trying to torture me. Can't they tell I need some space, time to think, time to put the house in some semblance of order? Don't they know that I can't do two things at once? Can't they just go five minutes without a request? How can it be that they need me so much?

—*Robin Ritchie, Salisbury, Maryland*

"It's For Your

My mother, like most mothers, had her own way of getting her point across. She always sat up and waited until I got home—no matter what time it was. It really bugged me, because it made me feel guilty.

I don't know how many times I tried to slip in late. There she would be, dressed in her robe, sitting in her rocker with a book or a Bible on her lap. "Thank God, you're all right," she'd say. That was it! She never lectured me or made threats.

"You don't need to wait up for me," I'd say sheepishly.

Mama would just smile, say goodnight, and go to her room. No matter how I begged her not to wait up for me, she was always there with the light on when I arrived.

As intent as I was on showing my independence and partying late if I wanted to, after a while Mama's night watchman routine got to me. I began to feel ashamed that Mama was losing sleep waiting up for me.

Own Good"

I knew my mother well enough to know that she was not going to change her ways, so I had to change mine. I finally just gave up and started coming home earlier. I ended up with a curfew—of my own making!

One morning Mama called me to get up for school. I had been out late the night before, and I didn't feel like budging.

My mother is a very unpredictable woman, and I'm sure I get plenty of my spunk from her. I was half-asleep, thinking she had given up on waking me. She quietly walked in my room, grabbed the overflowing ashtray by my bed, and dumped the cigarette butts and ashes all over my head.

"Now get up!" she said.

I jumped up, madder than a hornet. I could hear her laughing as she walked down the hall.

The next night I locked my door. The following morning Mama found a little firecracker of mine in her tool box, lit the fuse, and slid it under the door. To say the least, I sprang up thinking a terrorist car bomb had gone off.

Mama wasn't about to give up—neither was I. The next morning not only did I have the door locked, but I had wedged a wet bath towel into the crack under my door. I thought for sure I was safe from a firecracker blowing me out of bed. About that time, I heard Mama coming down the hall. I was in bed laughing to myself as I heard her jiggle the door handle and try to push some-thing under the door. I had outfoxed her this time.

But Mama, being the resourceful woman she is, persisted. All of a sudden I heard the window in my brother's room next door squeak open. I slid out of bed and peeked out the window. Here came Mama crawling on all fours across the roof! This time she was carrying a cup of water, which she had gripped in her teeth. I stifled a laugh. She was planning to douse me. Just as she got to my window, I grinned at her and said, "Sorry!" and slammed and locked the window. I stood there laughing and making faces at her as she peered into the window. There she was wondering what to do next. She reminded me of our cat with a dead mouse in its mouth, standing at the window wanting to come in.

She couldn't help herself—she grinned too, in spite of the cup. Because the roof had a fairly steep pitch, now she had to back up on all fours. It was a sight to behold! Suddenly, though, this wasn't so funny. I worried a little about her sliding off the roof, but it was obvious she was quite surefooted and would be okay. I made it to school on time that day too.

These confrontations with Mama weren't mean or bitter. On the one hand, my parents made it clear what they would accept or reject in my values and behavior. But on the other hand, they never squashed my individuality or demeaned me as a person. They knew much more clearly than I did the pressures I faced being a "preacher's kid" as well as the oldest son of a "Christian legend." I'm sure God gave them wisdom to know if they pushed me too hard to conform, I might take off running and never come back— not just from them, but perhaps from God too.

—Franklin Graham

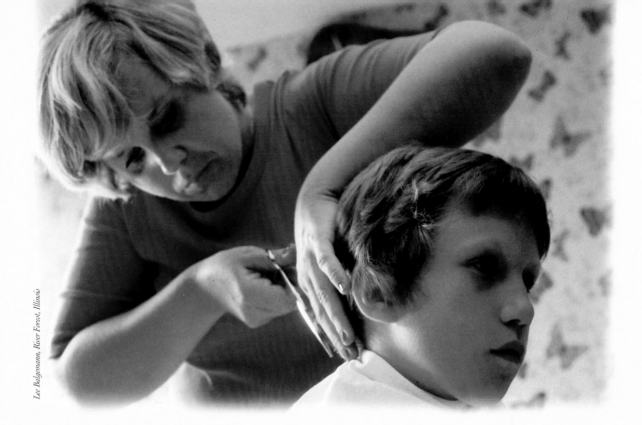

Lee Balgemann, River Forest, Illinois

I know I was a "no-nonsense" mom, which I learned from my own 1930s mother. I don't feel any guilt

having disciplined you children because you are now all generous, thoughtful people, and I thank God for "lending" you to me.

I have always felt richly blessed. I can leave this world knowing

I have left you with hearts full of love to thrive on, to spread around, and to enjoy.

Through the years we shared much happiness along with our trials. No mom could ask for more.

—Jean Garabrant, Amityville, New York

❧

I am continually amazed that my children will lick floors,

eat sand and bugs, float toys in the toilet, and share slobbered pacifiers,

but will not eat breaded chicken, mashed potatoes,

or those little friggly things in the soup.

—*Wendy Hyatt, Salem, New Hampshire*

❧

As a foster parent I find disciplining the toughest job of all. I've made a deliberate decision

to be firm and maintain a consistent stand regarding our moral values.

Our rules may be difficult for the child at the time, but they're better than

the life-damaging consequences which could appear later.

—*Beth Beasley, Ladson, South Carolina*

Being a young single mom is filled with tough times; pushing myself to cook dinner when I'm too tired to stand; having to go to the store for milk when I'm too sick to get up; worrying all night because my little one has such a high fever, knowing I have to go to work the next day. But then there are the good times too, the peace I feel when I'm rocking my sleeping daughter, feeling her love when she says, "I love you, Mommy," and seeing the incredible depth of her compassion when she cries because I'm hurting. Motherhood allows me to experience the most complete unselfish love. It takes a lot from me but it gives back so much more.

—*Cheryl Zantiny, Apple Valley, California*

April Saul/Philadelphia Inquirer, Philadelphia, Pennsylvania

Jeff Schultz, Anchorage, Alaska

DISCIPLINER

Dwight Cendrowski, Ann Arbor, Michigan

It is a rite of passage, of sorts. That letter. Or maybe a phone call. That moment when children take the last whack at the umbilical cord that connects them to their mothers.

I did it to my mother when I was thirty. Our children, one after another—born with too much '60s in them—were more precocious,

favoring me with the detailed list of my failings as a mother during their first or second year of college.

My response? Gulp, cry, get defensive, get angry, and finally admit—no, I wasn't perfect. Yes, I failed over and over again.

No, I didn't give you all you needed/wanted. But I did try.

—*Mary Ylvisaker Nilsen, Moorhead, Minnesota*

Hurry! hurry! hurry! . . . just hurry up!

What am I teaching you little one,

as I frantically run wild. . . .

Slow me down Lord. Quiet my heart.

Let me embrace this miracle right before my eyes.

—*Bonnie Knopf, Troutdale, Oregon*

Oh, it's so easy to be an armchair mother

and give excellent advice to others.

What a great mom I was before I had kids.

And now that my three sons are grown,

I'm once again such a wise mother.

It was the twenty-plus years in between

that rocked my confidence

and tested my sanity!

—*Claudia Arp, Knoxville, Tennessee*

Rachel LeCour, Atlanta, Georgia

"Wanna

M

My mother was a great handicap to me when I was little. She was different. I learned this very early, when I first began going to other children's houses. There, when the mother opened the door, she said something sensible like, "Wipe your feet" or "You're not bringing that junk in here."

At our house, however, when you rang the bell, the letter slot would open, and a little high voice would pipe out, "I'm the chief troll here. Is that you, Billy Goat Gruff?" Or a syrupy falsetto would sing the first few lines of "Barnacle Bill the Sailor": "Who's that knocking at my door?"

Other times the door would open a slit, and my mother, crouched down to our eye level would say, "I'm the new little girl here. Wait a minute, I'll call my mother." Then the door would close for a second, reopen, and there would be my mother—regular size. "Oh, hello, girls," she'd say. "I didn't know you were there."

Play?"

In that awful first moment when my new friend would turn to me with a "what kind of place is this?" look, I knew how it felt to open a closet and have the family skeleton sprawl all over you. "Mo-ther," I would bawl, but my mother would never admit to being the little girl who had opened the door. "You girls are kidding me," she'd say. We'd wind up protesting that a little girl had opened the door, when what we really meant was that no little girl had opened the door.

It was all very confusing. And different. That was the hard part. She was different from other mothers.

Like the seal in the basement.

When we were outside while my mother was washing or ironing in the basement, we would often hear a cheerful barking coming from down there. Mother's explanation was that it was our seal. Every Friday, she made a great show of unwrapping the fish (which eventually wound up on the dinner table) for the seal. And though kids made countless dashes down to the basement trying to catch the creature, he had always "just gone for a ride in the bakery truck" or "was taking his swimming lessons at the Y."

This seal was smart and would answer questions by barking once for "yes" and twice for "no." His reputation soon spread. Children came from blocks around to ask the seal questions at our basement window. The seal was always good for a few barks.

I was mortified to be pointed out as the girl with the seal, but my mother was equal to the occasion. Often when a crowd of little boys huddled at our window, waiting for a bark, my mother would open the door and call out gaily, "Hello, little girls."

My mother was no different with grownups. She often greeted an acquaintance by poking a finger in his back and growling, "Stick 'em up." The fact that adults liked my mother was no comfort to me. It was easy for them. She wasn't their mother.

Furthermore, they didn't have to put up with the "Interested Observer." My mother often carried on conversations about us with this invisible person.

"Would you look at the kitchen floor," my mother would say.

"Mud all over it and you just finished scrubbing it," the Interested Observer would say with sympathy. "Didn't you tell them to use the basement door?"

"Twice!"

"Don't they care how hard you work?" the I.O. wanted to know.

"I guess they're just forgetful."

"Well, if they'll get the clean rags under the sink and wipe it up, it'll help them to remember in the future," the I.O. would advise.

Immediately, we'd get the rags and go to work.

The Interested Observer's tone was so impartial nobody ever questioned his presence. He was so plainly there, observing family life and its problems, that friends never asked, "Who's your mother talking to?" but rather, "Who's that talking to your mother?"

I never found a suitable answer.

Luckily my mother improved with age. Not hers—mine. I was about ten the first time I ever realized that having a "different" mother could be a good thing.

The playground at the end of our street had a cluster of formidably high trees. To be caught climbing them brought out every mother for blocks, shrieking "Come down! You'll break your neck!"

One day, when a bunch of us were dizzily swaying in the top branches, my mother passed and caught sight of us silhouetted against the sky. We froze, but her face as she looked up was dazzling. "I didn't know you could climb so high," she shouted. "That's terrific! Don't fall!" And off she went. We watched in silence until she was out of sight. Then one boy spoke for us all. "Wow," he said softly. "Wow."

From that day on, I began to notice how my classmates stopped at our house before going home; how club meetings were always held in our kitchen; how friends, silent in their own homes, laughed and joked with my mother.

Later, my friends and I came to rely on my mother's light-hearted good humor as a support against adolescent crises. And when I began dating, it was wonderful to have a mother whom boys immediately adopted and a home where teenagers' craziness was not just tolerated, but enjoyed.

Everyone who knew my mother liked her. Many people loved her. All have said kind things about her. But I think the one who best described my mother was that boy, high in the tree, long ago.

"Wow," he said softly.

And I echo, "Wow."

—Jeanmarie Coogan

Doug Milner, Terrell, Texas

❧

I was playing "Ring Toss" with my seven-year-old granddaughter, Amanda, and we were keeping score.

I was called away from the game to take a phone call and wasn't watching as Amanda took her turn.

When I returned, she said she had scored many points.

I said fine, if she really did, but only God and she would know the truth.

She hesitated and then said, "You know what, let's start over!"

—*Judith H. Williams, Menomonee Falls, Wisconsin*

Dorothy Littell Greco, Boston, Massachusetts

Jonathan A. Meyers, Albuquerque, New Mexico

❧

I used to love watching my son

when he would go

to a park or playground.

He would run with

such grace and lightness

through the grass,

the sun shining in his hair.

It was like looking at

pure joy in motion.

— *Sharon Billings, Minneapolis, Minnesota*

❧

You brought me such joy, Sandra, and I loved you like my own daughter. You filled my days with laughter.

Remember that special day we took your drawings, the little duck eating corn and the cow

you had so carefully drawn with crayons, and we made a hooked rug? You were quite the artist at four.

You helped me choose the colored yarn and lay out the squares.

When we were finished, you laid your little head down on the rug and said over and over, "My duck."

Now forty-three years later you're all grown up, married with your own little girl.

You still have that funny little rug, and I still have the memory of your delightful expression,

the sparkle in your eyes, and the sound of your laughter.

— *Verna M. Nagy, Shell Beach, California*

❧

Being an older mom has its perks. You can actually feel good about spending money coloring your hair.

Best of all is the constant laughter that leaks out everywhere

as you watch your little cherub squeezing delight from every new discovery.

—*Ann Dunbar, Grand Rapids, Michigan*

Pastel bears and bunnies on the baby boy's crib.

Streamlined cobalt chassis buffed and polished to the hilt.

A grandson's dancing eyes, forlornly left behind,

Alas, the visit's over . . . care to guess my state of mind?

—*Gail Latimer, Union City, Tennessee*

It will never be said that Josh was an easy baby. But he was and is

the most loveable, sweet little boy. I love him so much.

—*Karen Higginbotham, Staten Island, New York*

Jerry Valente, Dedham, Massachusetts

Greg Schneider, Redlands, California

One goal we have for our family is that when the children are grown they continue to be friends.

I really believe that time spent playing with one another and having fun

is the glue that will hold their relationship together.

—*Terel Therkelsen, Mount Angel, Oregon*

ঽ

Sometimes I think the fighting will never end.

But once in a while, when the house becomes too quiet,

and I go searching for the boys and find them playing harmoniously together,

I'm really thankful that they have each other.

—*Kim Rosner, Phoenix, Arizona*

April Saul/Philadelphia Inquirer, Philadelphia, Pennsylvania

Children can't be children without fun, funning, funnies. And I need to remember to join in

on the hilarity and cherish their imaginations. Our making believe together is making memories,

creating the magic that imbues their happy childhood, leading them to a stable adulthood,

bringing them down the bunny trail to cradling their own children's dreams someday.

—*Kathy Burns, Chicago, Illinois*

From the moment you started crawling, I knew there were wild times ahead. If there was any child who loved critters and the outdoors, it was you, Robbie. What

fun we had playing explorer in the backyard. And as you grew, so did the adventures. Good thing I like critters too, else I would have flipped my lid the first time I

found the bathtub full of frogs or the turtle who took up residence in the dog's dish. But I think I laugh more over the time we turned the house upside down looking

for Checkers, your wily snake who came up missing, only to be discovered hiding behind the dishwasher! Even now that you're grown and on your own, I still find

myself tiptoeing around the house, wondering what little friend you've left behind . . .

—*Pat Nester, Palmdale, California*

Louis DeLuca, Dallas, Texas

Rina M. Gamasa, Santa Barbara, California

ᔥ

As you play, I watch your wonder and joy

at the simplest of things—the wind blowing leaves,

a hummingbird hovering over a flower.

Suddenly the whole world is put in perspective.

Thank you for reminding me

how good life really is.

—*Michelle Lewis, Phoenix, Arizona*

Barbara Maynard, Encinitas, California

ᔥ

I had fun with my kids when they were young—working together in the garden, building treehouses.

We even built our own home. Now all four kids have college degrees and are busy

creating on computers and helping to run our government. But guess what?

Now it's my thirty grandkids who want to build treehouses with Grandma.

—*Leone W. Fletcher, Provo, Utah*

"Let's

I suppose it was the reality of my first grandchild, Jamie, starting school that triggered the bittersweet memories of my first year of school. The year was 1942. Miss Edna was that marvelous old-fashioned kind of teacher who gladly put her entire life into teaching. I loved school: the smell of chalk and color crayons; the way the old wooden floors smelled after Jim the janitor had waxed them; and having my own desk that was just my size. There was, however, one overwhelming problem with school. Mildred.

Daily when I walked the short distance home after school, Mildred would taunt me, hit me, and scare me. I was absolutely terrified of her. She had failed first grade and was a year older than I. Mildred didn't have any friends, so she seemed to concentrate on making enemies. Because I was one of the smallest children in first grade she had selected me as her number one enemy.

Work It Out"

As we walked home after school, she would continually step on the back of the heels of my shoes and cause the shoes to slide down. Then, when I stopped to adjust them, Mildred would slap me hard on the back. As soon as the dismissal bell rang each day, my heart started to pound, and I blinked fast so I wouldn't cry.

Pretty soon my mother figured out something was wrong at school. I didn't want to tell her about

Mildred. I sat close to the radio listening to The Lone Ranger, pretending not to hear her questions about school. Mother continued to question me, and finally I sobbed out the whole story. "You can't do anything, Mama. You can't. Everyone will think I'm a baby."

It was impossible for Mother to pick me up after school. She had to work. My father had died a few years earlier. I didn't have any sisters or brothers to watch after me. I couldn't imagine what my mother might do. I was certain there was no answer—no answer at all for a problem this big.

The next day at school, Miss Edna leaned over my desk and whispered, "Marion, dear, could you stay after school and help me with a project? I spoke with your mother last evening and she said it would be fine with her." Her blue eyes were understanding, and she smelled like Jergens hand lotion. I decided right then that all angels must have blue eyes and smell like Jergens hand lotion. I nodded eagerly.

I remained joyfully at my desk when the dismissal bell rang. Mildred looked confused for a bit, but filed out with the others. After a while Miss Edna said that I'd better be going home. She stood on the front step of the school and waved to me. I skipped up the hill without any fear whatsoever. Then, just as I got to the top of the hill, I heard familiar footsteps behind me. Mildred had waited for me. She immediately stepped on the back of my shoe and slapped my back. I cried. I couldn't help it.

When my mother saw my face after she got home from work, she questioned me. I begged not to go to school and didn't sleep much that night. The next morning she said, "Marion, I'm going to walk up the hill with you today. I believe we'll see Mildred." Mildred walked from way across town to school. She never bothered me on the way to school, only afterward.

"Oh, Mama, please don't do that! Don't say anything to Mildred. It will just make her mad. Let me stay home by myself. Please, Mama."

"Hurry and get dressed, Marion." Her voice was gentle, but quite firm.

"Ple-e-ease, Mama."

"Trust me, Marion. I have a plan." My insides were in turmoil. Why couldn't my mother understand that no plan she had dreamed up was going to work? We bundled up against bitter cold and started walking up the hill. Maybe we wouldn't see Mildred, I hoped. But my mother had this confident look. I knew the look well, and I had a sinking feeling that we would see Mildred and that Mother would use her "plan."

Sure enough, just as we got to the top of the hill and I had to go in one direction to school and my mother in the opposite direction to her job at the bank, we spotted Mildred. We waited a few horrible moments as she approached us. She pretended not to see us, recognizing that I had my mother with me.

"Hello, Mildred," Mother said quietly. Mildred stopped, frozen as still as a statue. Her hands and face were bright red from the intense cold. Her oversized coat hung open. There were only two buttons on it. The rest were missing. Underneath she wore a cotton dress, as though it were summer. I was so wrapped up I could hardly walk. I even had to wear undershirts.

Mother stooped down to Mildred's level. She didn't say anything at first. Instead she rapidly buttoned Mildred's coat and turned the collar up around her neck. Then she fastened back this stubborn piece of hair that forever hung in Mildred's face. I stood off to one side watching our breath linger in front of our faces in the frigid morning air, praying that no students would happen by and that my mother's plan would be over quickly.

"I'm Marion's mother. I need your help, Mildred." Mildred looked intently at my mother with an expression I couldn't identify. Their faces were inches apart. My mother's gloved hands held Mildred's cold ones as she spoke. "Marion doesn't have any brothers or sisters. She sort of needs a special best friend at school. Someone to walk up the hill with her after school. You look like you'd be a fine friend for her. Would you be Marion's friend, Mildred?" Mildred chewed on her bottom lip, blinking all the time, and then nodded.

"Oh, thank you!" Mama said with certain confidence and gratitude. "I just know you are someone I can depend on." Then she hugged Mildred long and hard. She gave me a quick hug and called to us as though nothing unusual had happened. "Bye, girls. Have a good day." Mildred and I walked on to school, stiffly, like mechanical dolls, both staring straight ahead without speaking. Once I cut my eyes over her way. Mildred was smiling! I'd never seen her smile before.

We walked up the hill each day after school together, and pretty soon we were talking, laughing, and sharing secrets. Mildred started tying her hair back the way Mama had. Sometimes she even wore a hair ribbon. Someone sewed buttons on her coat, and she buttoned all of them and always wore the collar turned up. Somehow I started calling her "Mil." Then others did too, even Miss Edna.

"Hey, Mil, sit by me," someone called out at lunch. "No, Mil, sit with us," someone else begged. Mildred shot them a happy smile, but she always sat with me at lunch. My mother usually included something in my lunch especially for Mil—even notes of gratitude. Mil always let me get in front of her in the line at the water fountain.

Valentine's Day was a very important event in first grade back in the '40s. We made huge valentine boxes and set them on our desk for a valentine exchange. I pulled out an enormous valentine toward the end of the party. Everyone stood up to see better. It was store-bought! And it had obviously cost a lot. Most everyone had made their valentines from red construction paper, lace, and glue. *Ahhh's* and *ohhh's* floated out over the classroom and seemed to linger, suspended in the air, as I opened the magnificent valentine. Printed neatly in bold red letters inside the card was: "From your best friend."

I looked over at Mil. She was sitting with her hands folded on top of her desk and smiling the biggest smile ever. She had a red ribbon in her hair. Mildred smiled a lot now. She was getting good grades now, too, and didn't stuff her papers inside her desk anymore. Her eyes darted over and met mine. Right then I knew my mother's plan had worked.

I didn't understand Mama's plan back in 1942, or for years afterward. But along the way I discovered where my mother had gotten her remarkable plan. And I've learned that the plan works in all kinds of impossible situations: "Love is patient . . . kind . . . does not act unbecomingly . . . is not provoked . . . does not take into account a wrong suffered . . . believes all things . . . hopes all things . . . endures all things. Love never fails." (1 Corinthians 13:4-5, 7-8 NASB.)

—*Marion Bond West*

Jennifer George-Walker, San Diego, California

ॐ

Motherhood is a humbling experience. The challenges never end; they're just replaced by new ones.

My temper haunts me, and my outbursts forever ring in my own ears. But then, my daughter forgives her brother for breaking her toy,

or my son amazes me with an insight beyond his years. They have developed a new saying for each other.

"It's okay, pal." I wonder how they thought of that. Where did they learn this kind of forgiveness? Could I actually be doing some good for them?

Lord, I thank you for teaching my children through me, despite me.

—*Gail Lane, Bigfork, Montana*

"That's it. You're in for a time-out!" I say in my most authoritative-sounding Mommy voice—that is, after I've taken that well-known

Why the dreaded time-out works so well on my three-year old, who instantly displays contrition and remorse for his unacceptable behavior, astounds

—*Kimberly Carter, Bonita Springs, Florida*

I watch a young mother and her two very active,

noisy children a few booths down in this

nearly deserted small restaurant.

A few squabbles arise between the children,

and the mother becomes vocally abusive

and gives some shakings and spanks.

I wince. Should I stop and talk to her?

Should I tell her to be more affectionate,

more understanding?

That her whole satisfaction in life will depend

on those two tired, obviously bored, children?

—*Maxine Schweiker, Scottsdale, Arizona*

David Harrison, Topeka, Kansas

7 0

ep breath—my best defense against losing it completely.

. Too bad my mom didn't have this tool in her disciplining arsenal.

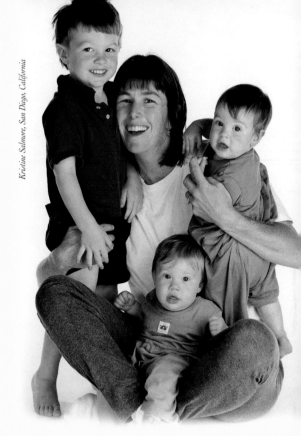

Kristine Salmore, San Diego, California

&

I'm forty-nine, with a son thirty-two and daughters nine and twelve. Twenty years between my first

two kids: two families, two lives, with this strangely familiar thread—me—running through.

As a second-time mother, I'm more patient, a little wiser, more humble, full of guilt.

My poor son—I was so young, so inexperienced, so confused, so confident! But look at him!

He's a wonderful, decent, sensitive man; he has reduced my guilt, increased my humility.

What wonderful gifts are my children, gifts that came with long,

unbreakable strings attached that both bind me and enable me to soar.

—*Diana L. Thrift, Takoma Park, Maryland*

❧

"Who do you love most?"

"I love both of you most."

"You can't love both of us most.

You have to love one of us more than the other."

"Okay, I love one of you more than the other."

"Which one, then?"

"Both of you?"

"I think you love her more than you love me."

"My sweetie, isn't this rather silly?

Is what you want for me to say that I love you most?"

"No! I want you to say that you love both of us most!"

"That's what I say!"

"Okay!"

—*Madeleine L'Engle, New York, New York*

Gary Fong, Castro Valley, California

"*Let Me*

I still hear the voice of my mother asking me what I see. I see a flower, a small flower. And she says, "Look at the colors, so pretty." Yes, a pretty flower. We were looking at daffodils in spring, the time to look closely at all that grows and all that begins to end.

My first teacher was my mother, a poet, a French-speaking Belgian immigrant, a reader, a holy woman who prayed, baked bread, endured great loneliness, loved the sound of the geese flying and the leaves shaking in the trees outside her window. She was a writer, friend, the wisest woman and the smartest woman I have ever met. My mother taught me how to recognize the smell of wisteria, how to feel the smooth shell of an egg against my cheek, how to button my shirt.

And it was from the hand of my mother when I was ten that I learned how to properly hold a spoon the first time I tried to feed my brother, Oliver—blind, mute Oliver, born without an intellect, in bed for thirty-two years incapable of learning anything.

"Chris, first let me show you how to make Oliver's dinner." It became my job to feed Oliver dinner.

"Take this red bowl," my mother said. "It is just the right size. Now, here, I use an egg," and she cracked an egg into the bowl. "Then I mix in just this much of baby cereal, sugar, and warm milk. Now mix this all together." I took a spoon and turned and turned the combined egg, milk, sugar, and cereal.

"Yuck!" I said, as I lifted the spoon out of the bowl and let some of the goop drip down.

Show You"

My mother smiled.

"Now, pour out a glass of milk, and let's go upstairs," she said.

My mother and I walked up the stairs as I carried the bowl of food and the glass of milk. Now that I look back, I realize how many times my mother had climbed those stairs up to Oliver's bedside. She climbed the mountain of labor and hope each day. Oliver could have defeated my mother, but instead, she turned the sugar, warm milk, and cereal into a meal and carried the bowl and glass up the stairs day by day. And she taught a small boy how to feed his brother, and that small boy, day after day, climbed those stairs too.

I remember that first night, when my mother explained the right way to feed Oliver. "Sit here, Chris, right beside him on the bed." As I sat next to my brother, I was afraid that my weight would shift Oliver's position and he would roll off the bed.

"It's okay, Chrissy." I looked up to my mother as she stood behind me. "Now, stir the food in the bowl one more time." I did. "Scoop up some food in the spoon." I dipped the silver spoon into the red bowl and came up with a mountain of goop. My mother didn't say anything. She let me figure out on my own that there was just too much on the spoon. Then she said, "Just think about feeding yourself. How much would you put on the spoon?"

I tried again, dipping the spoon into the mixture, and

then I did something that has stayed with me all my life. I tapped the side of the bowl to let some of the excess food spill from the spoon, and I heard the bowl ring a bit. The sound of a spoon knocking against a glass bowl is now a pure sound of recognition for me that something significant happened over thirty-five years ago when a mother stood over her two sons: the one who could not see, and the other who was just learning how.

"Now, Chris, place the spoon on Oliver's lips. Just a slight touch and see what happens."

I carried the spoon through the open air, across my lap, across his shoulders, and then, just as my mother said, I gently touched the tip of Oliver's lips with the spoon, and like a day lily, Oliver slowly opened his mouth. I looked back to my mother. She nodded. I saw what she wanted me to see: the hand of a human being bringing life to the lips of the powerless, humble, waiting child. And when Oliver opened his mouth for the food, I was delighted to see his response.

"Now, place the food in his mouth and let his lips scoop the food." And that is what I did. That is what Oliver did. And then he swallowed.

It was from the garden of my mother's heart where I learned how to love my brother, Oliver. A woman who has children has the power to nurture little seeds of life into full grown blossoms of existence. Oliver grew to the size of a ten-year-old. He had a large head and crooked legs. My mother taught me how to feed not only the distorted body of my brother, but also his purity of heart that he held deep within the roots of his existence.

Oliver is buried in a small cemetery in Weston, Vermont. I have his red dinner bowl on the shelf in this room where I write.

It is a reminder of that love and all that I learned from my mother, that I learned how to see and how to enter the garden of hope, tending to those we love with courage and compassion.

My mother taught me that. Courage and compassion.

—Christopher de Vinck

Mike Pattisall/Photri Inc., Falls Church, Virginia

&

I was going to save the world. I didn't.

Instead I have been saved through my children,

my beautiful children.

—*Catherine Deming-DeMars, Iowa City, Iowa*

Rina M. Ganassa, Santa Barbara, California

Kevin Vandivier, Austin, Texas

❧

I was complimenting

my daughters for

their work in charitable

organizations and was

surprised to hear

them reply,

"What do you expect?

Great-Grandma Ida taught

Grandma Ethel, and she

taught you.

We're just following

in the family footsteps."

—*Ruth Hirsh, Woodland Hills, California*

❧

I remember little toddler you, standing on a kitchen chair wearing a dish towel for an apron

as we washed dishes. "I'll rinse, Poo Poo," you told me. We splashed, stirred bubble soup, christened the kitchen

tongs a "batcatcher." Now you are seven and you proudly proclaim, "I can wash the dishes

all by myself!" You hold the knives very carefully and remind me to do the same. You have grown and changed so

much in five years, my sweet grandson, but the batcatcher will always be a batcatcher.

—*Rhoda Banta, Grand Rapids, Michigan*

TEACHER

Gutzen-Eye Press/Piotri Inc., Falls Church, Virginia

So much of our success in life, after all, is measured by how well we are able to get through the times that aren't so good—the times when we're too tired, when we're frightened, when we fail. If we are not around to serve as examples for our children, for how to get through those times and emerge victorious, then how will they learn the lesson? Few of us really are "born" for the job of mothering. . . . It means being willing to confront the worst in ourselves and being brave enough not to run away from it.

—*Linda Burton, Seymour, Illinois*

Heidi Bratton, Salem, New Hampshire

❧

Never did I imagine the depth of my mother's love for me until my Timothy was born. Now I truly understand the miracles of life and love.

—*Kristine Henderson, Kennesaw, Georgia*

❧

When I decided to
homeschool my son, Matthew,
I never expected to learn
so much about myself.
I was inexperienced
at teaching and
he certainly knew how
to push my buttons!
It was the best of times
and the worst of times.
But much more the best.
I treasure the special bond
we formed, the self-discipline
and patience we both
developed as we struggled
to reach the milestones.

—*Linda Errick, Umpqua, Oregon*

Jeff Schultz, Anchorage, Alaska

Now I know how wonderful it is to see my children doing an even better job of parenting than I did.

—Barbara Sibley, Des Plaines, Illinois

William B. Pope, Shawnee, Oklahoma

I always knew having kids would mean

constantly teaching them absolutely everything—

spiritual guidance, manners, language,

ambition, athletics—everything.

But when I was diagnosed with cancer,

I realized that a mother not only has to teach

her children how to live,

but we must, at some point, teach them

with dignity and faith, how to die.

—Meg Garland, Waco, Texas

It has finally occurred to me that my child

does not exist for me; does not say or do things

to please or displease me; but rather, because of me,

may be allowed to exist and to say and do enough

to reach a higher potential than she would without me.

—Judy Sirridge, Shawnee Mission, Kansas

Mothers are often wrong. When my ten-year-old son and I were in a store shopping,

he stopped to touch a computer display. I told him to get away, as he might break something.

With a big grin on his face he showed me his name, "Carlos," scrolling diagonally across the screen and,

with a touch of his finger, he reversed it from left to right and back again.

Guess who is now showing Mom how to use her new computer!

—Janet Gonzalez, Madison, Wisconsin

&.

Sensing my adult sons struggling,

I wonder what to do.

Mention it? Ask what's going on? Say nothing?

Look knowing and have them share their burdens?

Look carefree and hope they keep their problems to themselves?

Whatever I do, I want two messages to get across to them:

One, that I love them as much now

as I did when I was changing their diapers.

And two, that I love them differently now

—I respect the resources

God has placed within them to make wise decisions

without calling for Mom.

—Rachael Crabb, Morrison, Colorado

Barbara Maynard, Encinitas, California

Kevin Vandivier, Austin, Texas

Christopher Greco, Boston, Massachusetts

&.

How fortunate I am to have all three of you.

After two miscarriages and a difficult pregnancy, the miracle of your arrival, Chris,

was overwhelming. How could I ever part with you? Yet you, my firstborn, became your own person:

intelligent, sensitive, creative. Kelly, my determined child whose independence brought me both

frustration and pride, how could I not long to hold you close forever? Soon you will bring us our first

grandchild. May you, too, be blessed by a God-given independent child.

And you Carrie, my youngest, your strength and sensitivity were grown in the fertile valleys

of difficulty. How could I have forseen what a lovely, perceptive woman you would become? Each of

you has talents I never envisioned. But God did not mean for us to see

everything. You have learned from me, and now I am learning from each of you.

—Joan Capen, Rancho Santa Fe, California

I'm Here

Living as we did in a congested and bustling city, my mother arranged with a teenage girl who lived next door to walk me home at the end of the day. For this arduous responsibility, the girl was paid five cents a day, or a grand total of a quarter a week. In second grade, I became irritated that our poor family was giving this neighbor girl so much money, and I offered a deal to my mom. "Look," I said, "I'll walk myself to school and, if you give me a nickel a week, I will be extra careful. You can keep the other twenty cents, and we'll all be better off." I pleaded and begged, and eventually my mother gave in to my proposal. For the next two years I walked to and from school all by myself. It was an eight-block walk with many streets to cross, but I crossed them all with great care. I didn't talk to any strangers. I always kept on the appointed path. I always did as I promised, and I did it alone—or at least I thought I did.

For You"

Years later when we were enjoying a family party, I bragged about my characteristic independence and, in grandiose fashion, reminded my family of . . . the arrangements for going to and from school that I had worked out with Mom. It was then that my mother laughed and told me the whole story. "Did you really think you were alone?" she asked. "Every morning when you left for school, I left with you. I walked behind you all the way. When you got out of school at 3:30 in the afternoon, I was there. I always kept myself hidden, but I was there and I followed you all the way home. I just wanted to be there for you in case you needed me."

—*Anthony Campolo*

One morning when I was crying over the news of the death of a friend, and thinking of the pain her two little boys must be suffering,

my son, Alex, in his concerned toddler voice, asked me why I was crying.

I hugged him close and explained that someone very important and loved by many people had gone home to God.

He hugged me back and said, "No, Mommy, you're still here."

—*Dawn Chess, Glendora, California*

Geraldine Wilkins-Kasinga/
Los Angeles Times, Los Angeles, California

❧

We've waited so long for some word from you. Even as a young boy

you seemed such a lost little soul. Our prayers for you will never end.

—*Laura Branner, Fowlerton, Texas*

❧

At two o'clock in the morning I am awakened by the appearance

of a person no taller than a fire hydrant,

only his black eyes visible over the horizon of the mattress.

"What do you want?" I whisper. "Nothing," he whispers back. . . .

His search for reassurance leads him to our bed, where

two terribly fallible people toss and turn, the closest thing he knows to God.

—*Anna Quindlen, New York, New York*

❧

I pray my kids know you deeply (in spite of me).

For their sakes, Father, don't give up on me—change my heart!

Isaiah 40:11 "God gently leads those that have young" —lead me, Father.

—*Rhonda Johnson, Norman, Oklahoma*

Robert J. Pavuchak, Pittsburgh, Pennsylvania

☙

No matter what,

No matter when,

I hope you know

I'll always be here for you.

—*Betty Cantoni,*

San Diego, California,

☙

Today I didn't say the right things. I didn't give enough hugs. I didn't listen to all of their imaginary stories.

Today I hurried them through what could have been very special moments, to achieve my binding agenda.

Today my prayers were too short and my lectures too long. My smiles, I'm sure, didn't hide my fatigue.

Today I didn't heal any wounds; in fact, I'm sure I caused some. Their tears fell and I felt too lifeless to wipe them away.

Today I felt completely defeated and totally inadequate for this position called "mommy."

But as I kneel in prayer to confess my failures, I am reminded . . . I am not their hope. I am not their total joy. I am not their salvation. He is!

And they are his children even more than they are mine. I am reminded . . . He always listens, always guides, always touches, and always loves perfectly.

I can rest now, Lord, remembering that I am not alone.

—*Wendy C. Brewer, Fairview Heights, Illinois*

A MOTHER'S TOUCH

Gus Chan, Cleveland Heights, Ohio

⁊⸿

I know I cannot take the place of your mommy, but I love you boys,

all six of you, as my own. This road we're taking isn't easy, and I'm learning, too,

to be a stepmother, but we can work it out together, I promise. I'll listen.

I know it's difficult to accept new ways of doing things.

We'll make these changes together. Just know that I will always be here for you.

—Olivia Lainhart, Thayne, Wyoming

⁊⸿

You're sleeping now at last. . . .

Some days I think this nighttime peace

will never come. I love my days with you.

Your reliable smile was the only thing that lit

up this frantic house today, Max.

And, Zachary, I sometimes think

that if I had half your energy and persistence,

I'd accomplish miracles in minutes.

But loving my days with you as I do,

I have a motherly confession to make—

I love the hour you fall asleep as well.

—Mary Fisher, Nyack, New York

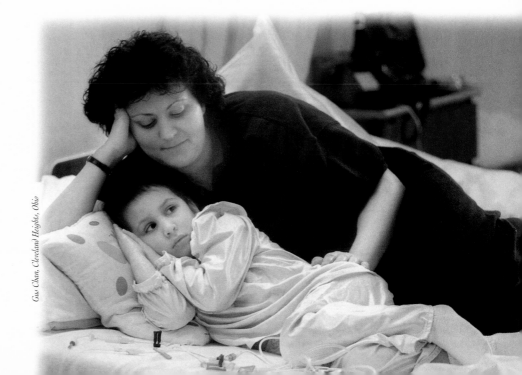

Gus Chan, Cleveland Heights, Ohio

CAREGIVER

❧

I'm twenty-five. I have five kids, two are not my natural children. I can't work, I have no friends,

and no real time with my hubby. I feel cheated sometimes. What happened to my career?

I spend every day just trying to get the kids through life. But I love being a mother. I do whatever it takes to make

sure all of my children, born to me or not, have the best life. This to me is being a mom, 'cause this is me and my life.

—*Sharon Lucas, Bentonville, Arkansas*

❧

Recess for my son is miserable. Not chosen for the sports teams,

yelled at and picked on, it's become an ordeal he faces daily.

I know this, I dread it for him, my heart aches. What can I do or say? How can I help?

When I tuck him in at night, rubbing his back as we talk,

I knead my comfort into him, and into me, too.

—*Mary Beth Lagerborg, Littleton, Colorado*

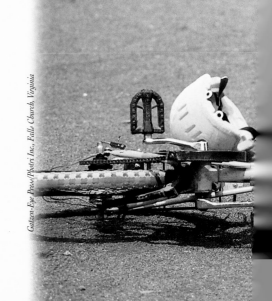

Suddenly I realize that the sheer intensity of my love cannot protect this child from the perils of life. Spinal meningitis.

Playground tragedies. Traffic accidents. God, I can't stand it. My chest constricts with unborn grief. My breath comes quickly.

To risk love is to risk loss. Shadows stretch across the living room and across my mind. And then I hear it. The still, small voice saying gently, deep inside,

"You're not a proud new owner. You're a trusted caretaker. This is my child, and I've lent him to you. Love him dearly, but hold him freely. Trust me for the days ahead."

—Sandra Bernlehr Clark, New Brighton, Minnesota

I'm thinking how little ones watch us from time to time just to see how we're reacting to the world news,

the death of a friend, the perpetuation of some gross injustice. Our children will reflect our reactions.

—Ruth Bell Graham, Montreat, North Carolina

Just being there in the morning when my children wake up enables them to know

I'm a regular part of their day and that I'm not going anywhere. Cameron will even ask the night before,

"Mom, will you put cereal out on the table with two bowls and two spoons?"

—Cheri Keaggy, Nashville, Tennessee

When my children are disobedient,

I see my disobedience. When they don't listen,

I recognize that I don't always listen.

When they don't ask first, I realize

I don't always ask first.

When I finally get totally exasperated with them,

I thank the Lord that he doesn't

give up on any of us!

—Kathy Mounts, Broken Arrow, Oklahoma

I've been pulled from all sides taking care of my mother-in-law, helping my own children and their children.

But of great concern to me is what will happen when I lose the ability to care for my own needs, and I wonder who will take care of me.

—*Joanie Richeson, Estes Park, Colorado*

Dwight Cendrowski, Ann Arbor, Michigan

Sometimes talking to Mother was like talking to a stone. Her jaw was set, her voice hard. "You can't go outside and play until you learn your times tables."

Mother wasn't home, of course, when school let out, but it didn't occur to me to disobey. She had taught Curtis and me properly, and we did what she told us.

I learned the times tables. I just kept repeating them until they fixed themselves in my brain. Like she promised, that night Mother went over them with me. Her constant interest and unflagging encouragement kept me motivated.

Within days after learning my times tables, math became so much easier that my scores soared. Most of the time my grades reached as high as the other kids in my class. . . .

Things changed immediately and made going to school more enjoyable. Nobody laughed or called

Do It!" me the dummy in math anymore! But Mother didn't let me stop with memorizing the times tables. She had proven to me that I could succeed in one thing. So she started the next phase of my self-improvement program to make me come out with the top grades in every class. The goal was fine, I just didn't like her method.

"I've decided you boys are watching too much television," she said one evening, snapping off the set in the middle of a program.

"We don't watch that much," I said. I tried to point out that some programs were educational and that all the kids in my class watched television, even the smartest ones.

As if she didn't hear a word I said, she laid down the law. I didn't like the rule, but her determination to see us improve changed the course of my life. "From now on, you boys can watch no more than three programs a week."

"A week?" Immediately I thought of all the wonderful programs I would have to miss. . . .

Mother had already decided how we would spend our free time when we weren't watching television. "You boys are going to go to the library and check out books. You're going to read at least two books every week. At the end of each week you'll give me a report on what you've read."

That rule sounded impossible. Two books? I had never read a whole book in my life, except those they made us read in school. I couldn't believe I could ever finish one whole book in a short week.

But a day or two later found Curtis and me dragging our feet the seven blocks from home to the public library. We grumbled and complained, making the journey seem endless. But Mother had spoken, and it didn't occur to either of us to disobey. The reason? We respected her. We knew she meant business and knew we'd better mind. But, most important, we loved her.

"Bennie," she said again and again, "if you can read, honey, you can learn just about anything you want to know. The doors of the world are open to people who can read. And my boys are going to be successful in life, because they're going to be the best readers in the school."

As I think about it, I'm as convinced today as I was back in the fifth grade, that my mother meant that. She believed in Curtis and me. She had such faith in us, we didn't dare fail! Her unbounded confidence nudged me into starting to believe in myself.

—Ben Carson

Patrick Davison, Westminster, Colorado

Chris Clark/The Grand Rapids Press, Grand Rapids, Michigan

My son has struggled with epilepsy and debilitating headaches since he was a toddler.

There were many days when we both just cuddled together on the couch and cried.

I felt so helpless because I couldn't ease his pain, nor mine.

I thought I knew what courage was, but my son has taught me better.

His challenges have helped me grow stronger, more patient, more loving.

His triumphs are my heart's reward. I am so proud of him.

—*Linda Nylin, Sacramento, California*

After my first child, I thought

I knew everything about being a mother.

My second child taught me otherwise.

—*Victoria Cendrowski, Ann Arbor, Michigan*

ENCOURAGER

Patrick Davison, Westminster, Colorado

Today I forgot to pick up

my child at the bus stop.

I can't believe I did that!

Keeping up with a family, a job,

and my own life is tiring.

I try, but sometimes I don't

feel like I'm a very good mom.

—*Julia Whitworth,*

San Diego, California

Dwight Cendrowski, Ann Arbor, Michigan

Being Abigail's grandmother is my privilege.

The world is a harsh place for little ones in wheelchairs; people don't always see Abigail.

But Abigail knows I see her for who she is in all of her amazing uniqueness.

—*Debra Evans, Austin, Texas*

A MOTHER'S TOUCH

❧

When each of you precious babies were placed

in my arms, I prayed that you both

would grow into fine adults. But raising you

was a rougher road than I expected.

There were times I felt I really was at the end

of my rope, struggling to get you through

the toy tug of wars,

the squabbles over who ate the last of the cereal,

and your explosive tempers

and posturing displays during your teens.

I felt like I wanted to run away from home myself,

but all I could do was tie another knot

and hang in there.

But God smiled on me. You both are now fine men

with families of your own.

I'm sure glad I hung in there.

—Arline Nester, Thousand Oaks, California

❧

I have to remember to be my children's cheerleader! If they aren't getting praise and encouragement at home,

they are probably having to do without because no one else cares enough to give it.

I want our home to be a haven, a place where they are accepted, loved, and respected as a special gift of God.

—Nancy Dunn, Union City, Tennessee

Greg Schneider, Redlands, California

❧

So many times I've wanted to save my son the struggle of completing a difficult task by doing it for him.

Instead, I've tried to offer encouragement and express my confidence in his abilities.

Standing by, letting him find his own way, is the more difficult task for me.

The reward: this self-sufficient young man I now see before me.

—*Brooke Kirby, Del Mar, California*

❧

I can barely see my daughter among

the rows and rows of clarinets.

The first notes begin, blaring yet timid,

slightly out of tune and tempo.

Magically though, to a mother's ears

it is the sweetest symphony.

My thoughts race back thirty years,

and I see my mother in the audience,

her hands fluttering with the loudest clapping,

as mine are now.

—*Beverly Joblin, Iowa City, Iowa*

Kevin Vandivier, Austin, Texas

Our daughter's graduation from high school depended on whether she got a D in math or an F. As we waited to learn the outcome, I was distraught,

certain her future was ruined. Today, she's a successful businesswoman. Even more impressive are her kind, generous spirit

and delightful sense of humor. As a teenager she gave us glimpses of those qualities, but I could only focus on her failure to achieve.

Fortunately, our children are often able to overcome our shortsightedness.

—Nancy Werking Poling, Evanston, Illinois

It'll Make

Coming home from school that dark winter's day so long ago, I was filled with anticipation. I had a new issue of my favorite sports magazine tucked under my arm, and I'd have the house to myself. Dad was at work, my sister was away, and Mother wouldn't be home from her new job for an hour. I bounded up the steps, burst into the living room, and flipped on a light.

I was shocked into stillness by what I saw. Mother, pulled into a tight ball with her face in her hands, sat at the far end of the couch. She was crying. I had never seen her cry.

I approached cautiously and touched her shoulder. "Mother?" I said. "What's happened?"

She took a long breath and managed a weak smile. "It's nothing, really. Nothing important. Just that I'm going to lose this new job. I can't type fast enough."

You Stronger"

"But you've only been there three days," I said. "You'll catch on." I was repeating a line she had spoken to me a hundred times when I was having trouble learning or doing something important to me.

"No," she said sadly. "There's no time for that. I can't carry my end of the load. I'm making everyone in the office work twice as hard."

"They're just giving you too much work," I said, hoping to find injustice where she saw failure. She was too honest to accept that.

"I always said I could do anything I set my mind to," she said. "And I still think I can in most things. But I can't do this."

I felt helpless and out of place. At age sixteen I still assumed Mother could do anything. . . .

"I guess we all have to fail sometime," Mother said quietly. I could sense her pain and the tension of holding back the strong emotions that were interrupted by my arrival. Suddenly, something inside me turned. I reached out and put my arms around her.

She broke then. She put her face against my shoulder and sobbed. I held her close and didn't try to talk. I knew I was doing what I should, what I could, and that it was enough. In that moment, feeling Mother's back racked with emotion, I understood for the first time her vulnerability. She was still my mother, but she was something more: a person like me, capable of fear and hurt and failure. I could feel her pain as she must have felt mine on a thousand occasions when I had sought comfort in her arms.

Then it was over. Wiping away the tears, Mother stood and faced me. "Well, son, I may be a slow typist, but I'm not a parasite and I won't keep a job I can't do. I'm going to ask tomorrow if I can finish out the week. Then I'll resign."

And that's what she did. Her boss apologized to her, saying he had underestimated his workload as badly as she has overestimated her typing ability. They parted with mutual respect, he offering a week's pay and she refusing it.

A week later Mother took a job selling dry goods at half the salary. . . . "It's a job I can do," she said simply. But the evening practice sessions on the old green typewriter continued. I had a very different feeling now when I passed her door at night and heard her tapping away. I knew there was more going on in there than a woman learning to type.

When I left for college two years later, Mother had an office job with better pay and more responsibility. I believe that in some strange way she learned as much from her moment of defeat as I did, because several years later, when I had finished school and proudly accepted a job as a newspaper reporter, she had already been a reporter with our hometown paper for six months.

Mother and I never spoke again about the afternoon when she broke down. But more than once, when I failed on a first attempt and was tempted by pride or frustration to scrap something I truly wanted, I would remember her selling dresses while she learned to type. In seeing her weakness I learned not only to appreciate her strengths, I discovered some of my own.

—*Gerald Moore*

Jerry Valente, Dedham, Massachusetts

&

I keep telling myself I should be able

to organize better, choose more wisely,

handle children and deadlines

with more patience. . . .

"Gigi," I tell myself, "you don't need

to live in this state of semipanic.

You don't need to wake up feeling so

wired each morning."

. . . Which battles are really worth

fighting? Is it worth all the emotional

effort to make the kids eat their peas?

With my first child I decided it was.

I would put the peas in his mouth,

then hold his mouth shut

until he swallowed them.

Six children later, I've decided

it is not worth the battle.

—*Gigi Graham Tchividjian, Miami, Florida*

&

My college classmates, my peers, are in the prime of their careers.

They travel the globe, speak at national conferences, and win prestigious awards.

I push the double stroller to the tot lot, take my turn leading play group,

and glue seven different kinds of macaroni noodles on my son's artwork.

Their work appears on the covers of magazines.

My work crawls, sleepy-eyed, into bed with us at 6:30 A.M. demanding, "Play with me."

I've struggled to get to a place of peace and contentment with this phase in my life.

My faith and my family are my life now. What is a career anyway but one's life work?

—*Dorothy Littell Greco, Boston, Massachusetts*

It was one of those days. Pouring rain outside; everyone was sick, overtired, feverish, and crabby. My one-year-old cried all day,

screamed rather, and he was permanently attached to my left hip. My three-year-old delighted, it seemed, in defying,

disobeying, picking on her brother, messing up the house, slamming doors, and generally wearing me down!

These are the days I call my own mother. "I really don't think I can do this anymore," I moan into the phone.

She smiles, listens, and empathizes. She, as my mother, spends a moment understanding the mother in me.

Two hours later a bouquet of pink roses arrives at my door, a "hug" of hope and encouragement from my mother six states away.

—Wendy Egan, Wayzata, Minnesota

❧

When I started to work again after being home with my son,

I was so surprised by the renewed energy in my life.

There was a side of me that I had lost touch with.

Now I love being there for him, but I also love my work.

I feel more balanced and energized because of it.

—Mo Latimer, San Diego, California

❧

Caring for my three preschoolers meant

tending to endless tasks 24 hours a day, 7 days a week.

I realized early on that if I didn't take care of the caregiver,

no one's needs would be met. Periodically, I would lock

myself in my bedroom to rest or savor a quiet moment.

It took only minutes before they were pounding on my door

asking what I was doing. Since they were too young to

understand the complexities of motherhood,

I would simply say, "I'm making you a better mom!"

—Rebekah Marshall, Monroe, New York

Louis DeLuca, Dallas, Texas

❧

I feel disappointed at how quickly my patience can be stripped

from me. I thank God for the fresh start each morning offers me.

—*Vonda Kay Schaefer, Buelton, California*

❧

I wonder, my darling children, if you know that

every night when you were small

I would go to each of your rooms and quietly

pray to the Lord as you lay sleeping

that you would grow up to be responsible

adults and good citizens.

—*Jean Kunkel, San Jose, California*

Doug Hopfer, Garland, Texas

My heart looks different from when my first child was born. Then it was fresh and new.

Now it's scarred and worn, but it's larger, more tender.

—*Kelly Jacobson, Lone Tree, Colorado*

David Lacey, Golden Valley, Colorado

"I'm the mom, that's why!"

Those words still echo in my mind. I tried to be a patient

mom. Tried to explain "why" it was important to do what I

asked, but there were days when my patience stretched no

futher than that! I wondered if my daughter would ever

understand. Now, after forty years of watching her raise her

four boys—and run herd over her eight grandchildren—

she'll catch my glance and whisper to me, "Now I know!"

—*Evelyn Weyand, Reno, Nevada*

"Tell Me

My period was late, but I didn't think too much about it. I just knew I couldn't be pregnant. Surely that couldn't happen to me.

Mom knew about the relationship I had with my boyfriend. It was clear that she disapproved. We'd had many talks about sex, and I knew that she believed God's plan for sexual intimacy was that it be saved exclusively for marriage. But I just couldn't see the reasoning behind her thinking—or at least I didn't want to. I knew Mom was worried about me, and that both bothered and annoyed me because we were close.

Finally she said to me, "Stacy, do you think you could be pregnant? I think you should take a pregnancy test."

Her comment really shook me because I was beginning to wonder myself. Summoning up courage, I decided to follow her advice. It was a busy weekend for our family. Mom and Dad had taken our out-of-town company sightseeing, and I was finally alone and able to do the test. I was anxious as I waited for the results. When I saw the clear positive sign I almost threw up. Nervous, badly frightened, and in tears, I curled up on the couch and waited for Mom to come home. I felt so ashamed. I knew how devastated my parents were going to be. . . . I was in agony. What would I do?

All About It"

What would Mom say?

Mom's response was amazing. She held me in her arms and let me cry. Her response was, "Stacy, we will get through this."

She could have said, "I told you so." She could have gone on about how I'd let her and Dad down, how I had disobeyed God, how I had messed up my life. But she didn't.

Instead we began a difficult journey—but we began it together. Mom and Dad didn't pressure me into any decision. They listened, they prayed for me, and they guided me to resources to help me. We all knew that I had to make the difficult decisions about the pregnancy and this child. With their full support I went to Liberty Home for Unwed Mothers in Lynchburg, Virginia.

Mom wrote almost every day. She called. She visited me at every opportunity. And she prayed. When I made the decision to give the baby up for adoption, she supported me.

When the time came for me to deliver, Mom was there. She stayed with me throughout a long, difficult labor and delivery. It was hard for me, but it was even harder for Mom because the day I went into labor, her own mother became ill and died. Yet she chose to stay with me because she felt I needed her most.

Having decided that it was best to give up my baby, I knew I couldn't even hold her when she was born or I might change my mind. So it was Mom who stood in for me and in whose arms the doctor placed my baby girl.

The day of my daughter's birth was a day of double loss for Mom—the day she had to give up her first and only grandchild and the day she lost her mother. But it was a day I knew, as never before, that she loved me. She stood by me, she forgave me, and she loved me unconditionally. Because of her example, I am able to accept God's forgiveness and to believe in his unconditional love for me.

—*As told to Susan Alexander Yates and Allison Yates Gaskins*

Alvin Gee, Houston, Texas

Dorothy Littell Greco, Boston, Massachusetts

❦

Just when you think your children

are grown and don't need you anymore,

they call.

—Nancy Fay, Pittsburgh, Pennsylvania

❦

Thanks for teaching me to listen. For only by listening to the words you speak have

I been able to realize how much we have taught and shared with each other.

What a spectacular, priceless gift. I love you!

—Susan Shaw, Shiremanstown, Pennsylvania

Lil Jonas, Hazleton, Pennsylvania

ॐ

My sons at 3 and 4:

Mom, I need a "conbersation"—

off we went to a quiet place to discuss what was so urgent.

My sons at 27 and 28:

Mom, I need a "conbersation" (a true term of endearment).

I'm so glad I listened.

—*Linda M. Repsher, Carlsbad, California*

Bounding in, bursting with excitement,

bubbling with laughter, recounting her time away—

I love the first few moments when

my child returns after being away.

—*Mary Bryne Santori, Northridge, California*

Being a recovering addict has taken its toll on us,

but I now have a relationship with my daughters, and for the first time,

I can see trust in their eyes. I never want to lose that trust again.

—Laura Romero, Sacramento, California

It's so hard to catch up with my teenagers these days.

They're always running off to somewhere.

I've made a real point to stay flexible so I can be available when they need me.

Some of our most meaningful times have occurred when I least expected it.

—Lynn Swenson, Seattle, Washington

❧

When my children were little, I thought it important to be home for them

when they got home from school. But now that they are in high school

it's even more important. I know it is the best way I can spend my time these days.

Soon they will be off on their own. I want to be confident that

I did all I could to help them off to a good start.

—Patty Brockhaus, Encinitas, California

❧

You and I see things differently since the divorce. You just want things to be

like they were before. I know you hurt deep inside. (Your malevolence spills

over everyone on visitation weekends.) For me, I've been through so much

pain, I just want things to be peaceful, productive, and full of joy. Perhaps we

will both understand each other someday as we look back on this "hang in

there" time in all our lives. Remember I love you!

—ML Chandler, Sonora, California

Remember

Quite often my mother would ask me to set the family table with "the good china." As is often the case, china was a family heirloom, passed down from generation to generation and held in the highest regard. My mother ordered the table to be set with the china quite frequently, but I never questioned these occasions. I assumed they were just my mother's desire or momentary whims and did what I was asked.

One evening as I was setting the table, our neighbor, Marge, dropped by unexpectedly. She knocked at the door and Mom, busy at the stove, called to her to come in. Marge entered the large kitchen and, glancing at the beautifully set table, remarked, "Oh, I see you're expecting company. I'll come back another time. I should have called first, anyway."

"No, no, it's all right," replied my mother. "We're not expecting company."

"Well then," said Marge, with a puzzled look on her face, "why would you have the good china out? Gosh, I'd never trust my son to handle my grandmother's dishes. I'm so afraid they'll get broken, I use them only twice a year, if that."

"Because," my mom answered, laughing softly, presumably because she found it silly that Marge should use her china so infrequently, "I've prepared my family's favorite meal. If you set your best table for guests and outsiders when you prepare a special meal, why not for your own family? They're as special as anyone I can think of."

"Well, yes, but your beautiful china will get chipped," responded Marge, still not understanding the importance of the value my mother had assigned to esteeming her family in that way. "And then you won't have it to pass on to your children."

"Oh well," said Mom, casually, "a few chips in the china are a small price to pay for the joy we get using it. Besides," she added with a twinkle in her eyes, "all these chips have a story to tell, now don't they?" She looked at Marge as though a woman with a family of her own should have known this.

Marge still didn't get it.

Mom walked to the cupboard and took down a plate. Holding it up, she said, "See this chip? I was seventeen when this happened. I'll never forget that day." My mother's voice softened, and she seemed to be remembering another time. "One fall day my brothers needed help putting up the last of the season's hay, so they hired a strong young man to help out." Mom paused, then continued. "My mother had asked me to go to the hen house to gather fresh eggs. It was then when I first noticed this very handsome young man. I stopped and watched for a moment as he picked up the large and heavy bales of freshly cut hay and slung them up and over his shoulder, tossing them effortlessly into the hay loft. I tell you, he was one gorgeous man: lean, slimwaisted, with powerful arms and shiny, thick sandy-blond hair. He must have felt my presence because with a bale of hay in midair, he stopped and turned and looked at me, and just smiled. He was so incredibly handsome," she said slowly, running a finger around the plate, stroking it gently.

"Well, I guess my brothers took a liking to him because they invited him to have dinner with us. When my older brother directed him to sit next to me at the table, I nearly fainted. You can imagine how embarrassed I felt because he had seen me standing there staring at him. Now, here I was seated next to him. His presence made me so flustered, when he asked me when I was to graduate, I got tongue-tied. I don't remember what I said!" Suddenly remembering that she was telling a story in the presence of her young daughter and a neighbor, Mom blushed and hurriedly brought the story to conclusion. "Well, anyway, he handed me his plate and asked that I dish him a helping. I was so nervous that my hands shook. When I took his plate, it slipped and cracked against the casserole dish, knocking out a chip. I handed the plate back to him, hoping he hadn't noticed."

"Well," said Marge, unmoved by my mother's story, "I'd say that sounds like a memory I'd try to forget."

"On the contrary," countered my mother. "As he was leaving the house he walked over to me, took my hand in his and laid the little piece of chipped glass in my palm. He didn't say a word, just smiled that incredible smile. One year later I married that marvelous man. And to this day, when I see this plate, I fondly recall the day I met him." She carefully put the plate back into the cupboard—

behind the others, in a place all its own. Seeing me staring at her, she gave me a quick wink. . . .

I was sure my mother had other stories to tell about that set of china.

Several days passed and I couldn't forget about that plate with the chip in it. That plate had been made special, if for no other reason than because Mom had stored it carefully behind the others. There was something about that plate that intrigued me, and thoughts of it lingered in the back of my mind.

A few days later my mother took a trip into town to get groceries. As usual, I was put in charge of caring for the other children while she was gone. As she drove out of the driveway, I did what I always did in the first ten minutes when she left for town: I ran into my parents' bedroom (as I was forbidden to do!), pulled up a chair, opened the top dresser drawer and snooped through it, as I had done many times before. There in the back of the drawer and beneath soft and wonderful smelling grown-up garments, was a small, square, wooden jewelry box. I took it out and opened it. Inside were the usual items, the red ruby ring left to my mother by Auntie Hilda, her favorite aunt; a pair of delicate pearl earrings given to my mother's mom by her husband on their wedding day; and my mother's dainty wedding ring, which she often took off as she helped do outside chores alongside her husband.

Once again enchanted by these precious keepsakes, I did what every little girl is wont to do. I tried them all on (as I had done so many times before), filling my mind with glorious images of what I thought it must be like to be grown up, to be a beautiful woman like my mother and to own such exquisite things. I couldn't wait to be old enough to command a drawer of my very own and be able to tell others they could not go into it!

Today I didn't linger too long on these thoughts. I removed the fine piece of red felt from the lid on the little wooden box that separated the jewelry from an ordinary-looking chip of white glass, heretofore completely meaningless to me. I removed the piece of glass from the box, held it up to the light to examine it more carefully and following an instinct, ran to the kitchen cabinet, pulled up a chair, climbed up and took down that plate. Just as I had guessed, the chip so carefully stored beneath the only three precious keepsakes my mother owned, belonged to the plate she had broken on the day she had first laid eyes on my father.

Wiser now, and with more respect, I cautiously returned the sacred chip to its place beneath the jewels and replaced the piece of fabric that protected it from being scratched by the jewelry. Now I knew for sure that the china held for Mother a number of love stories about her family, but none quite so memorable as the legacy she had assigned to that plate. With that chip began a love story to surpass all love stories, now in its fifty-third chapter—for my parents have been married now for some fifty years!

One of my sisters asked Mother if someday the antique ruby ring could be hers, and my other sister had laid claim to Grandmother's pearl earrings. I want my sisters to have these beautiful family heirlooms. As for me, well, I'd like the memento representing the beginning of a very extraordinary woman's very extraordinary life of loving; I'd like that little glass chip.

—*Bettie B. Youngs*

John Gilroy, Kalamazoo, Michigan

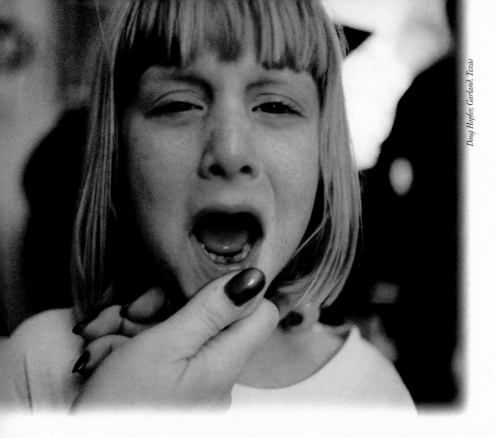

Doug Hopfer, Garland, Texas

❧

My connection with Mama on my birthday had
always been very special, and, of course, entirely
personal between the two of us. On my birthday, a
month after she died, as I opened and read birthday
greetings from family and friends, I searched through
the envelopes looking for a birthday card from my
mother, and when I did not find one—only then did
the reality of her death grip me. Today, my throat
tightens and my eyes brim when I remember the
heartbreak long ago on my forty-second birthday—
the day I knew with unerring certainty
that Mama had died.

—*Ruby Minatre Ott, Longview, Texas*

❧

It was just a glimmer of an expression, but when
Will rolled over and made that face, my mind flashed back
to the days when Tricia, his mother, was that age.
I had to run and get out the photo album—
sure enough, there was that same smile.
Oh, being a Gramma is so much fun!

—*Mary Grame, San Diego, California*

Louis DeLuca, Dallas, Texas

I can't remember exactly when either of my daughters first said,

"I love you," but even now they never fail to say it before

hanging up the phone or when leaving me.

They are both in their 20s. I am now a grandmother

and my three-year old granddaughter said to me one day,

"I uv you , Damma." My heart melted. I'll never forget that day.

She still gives wonderful hugs and tells me she loves me.

The words, *love* and *Grandma* are spoken clearly now

but, in my heart I still hear, "I uv you, Damma."

—*Lou Ellen Chilton, San Diego, California*

Dwight Cendrowski, Ann Arbor, Michigan

1989

1991

1993

Georgia Lippincott and Susan Phillips, Del Mar, California

❧

As I have gone through

the days of motherhood with

the three of you (19, 16, 13)

and look back, I see

that the joys you gave me

are the things I remember most.

There were harder struggles

as you grew each year

but they did pass.

God's love for us is amazing!

The problems encountered

in childhood are just a tiny spot

in our memories

compared to my heart full of

wonderful memories that are

still being made day by day.

Thank you, my precious

children!

—*Sue Durkes, Denver, Colorado*

Tom Watson, Skaneateles Lake, New York

❧

I look at you on your thirty-first birthday and see a man,

and I'm surprised. I have always thought of you as my son,

a child to encourage and help grow.

But you are grown and somehow I didn't realize it.

I talk to you now and know that I must have done

a good job. Or is it that I still see you

through a mother's eyes?

—*Phyllis Dugan, Thayne, Wyoming*

1 2 7

I can still remember walking into your kitchen and standing there, a nervous, skinny eighteen-year-old, wondering what you would say to me after you had received Johnny's telegram telling you he was bringing me home—his new wife. You just looked at me, but your eyes gave me hope. You embraced me with love, took me under your wing, and nurtured me as a daughter. You shared your life with me— taught me so many things, to crochet, to make bread, and to cook a hundred Italian dishes—from scratch. You were always there for me, my confidant, my friend. You helped me raise my two babies. And now some fifty-five years later as I look around my home, your love still embraces me.

Mom, I miss you.

—Jean O. Santori, Northridge, California

Jeff Schultz, Anchorage, Alaska

Etched in my heart forever are the countless moments—Dad's surprise fiftieth, finally having to tell Kris about Santa, the duck joke, John's slide down Mt. Washington, Becky's taking the wrong bus home from kindergarten. Yes, I miss them. Oh, but what added rewards to see each of them grown, mature, productive, and loving, and expanding our family in beautiful ways!

—Clara E. Kennedy, Westford, Massachusetts

A MOTHER'S TOUCH

Kevin Vandivier, Austin, Texas

While rummaging through the garage today, I bumped into our old canoe. It teetered slightly and down fell one of the paddles. Suddenly my mind flooded with memories of when you kids were little and of all the summers we spent together playing in that canoe. Friends thought us crazy taking you children backcountry canoeing, but we had such fun. Remember when we celebrated your twelfth birthday, Blair, floating down the Yukon River—how we laughed passing birthday cake from one to the other on canoe paddles. You kids are all grown and on your own now, but you still talk about that trip as if it were only yesterday. Wasn't it?

—*Sandra Gillespie, San Luis Obispo, California*

David Lacey, Golden Valley, Colorado

❧

Mommy, I remember thinking I'd never be like you when I had kids, but my little girl and I are just like you! She's stuck to me as you said I was stuck to you. So often I wish you were here so that I could ask you, "what was I like then?" or "what did you do when?" Instead, I rely on others, and myself, learning as I go. But I know you're watching my little girl and me, and I'm glad.

—*Nadene Eisner-Saywitz, Naperville, Illinois*

೩•

Slipping his small hand into my open palm, simultaneously filling my hand and heart. His requests,

"Can you hold me, Mama?" I was prepared for those encounters: the unconditional love, the

nurturing feelings, the closeness. What surprised me were the early, continual attempts at moving

away from mom. At two, pushing my hand away—stating, "Mine do it." Later, waving a confident

good-bye as he left for kindergarten in clothes he chose.

—*Barbi Townsend, Newport Beach, California*

A MOTHER'S TOUCH

❧

Now that you are almost grown I look back and ask myself, Did I tell you?

Did I tell you all that I meant to tell you, all that I felt was important?

Did I tell you or was it lost in the shuffle of our everyday lives?

The busy full days when we taught and didn't know it. What did we teach? Was it strong?

Was it good? Will it root you in something real that will allow you to grow with a firm and sound foundation? . . .

Did I tell you to laugh, to dance, to sing?

There is a lot in life that is hard, but take it as it comes and find the good

. . . and make time to dance.

—*Elizabeth Knapp, Fresno, California*

Ron Nickel, Three Hills, Alberta

I'll

I

I miss my mom.

There, I've said it. One small sentiment that has the power to ravage a college girl's reputation.

Surely my emotional growth, which should have been completed in the three short months between high school graduation and freshman orientation, must have been stunted somehow. Why else would I spend college—my ticket out of a tedious existence of walking the dog, emptying the dishwasher twelve times a day, and being my sister's unpaid chauffeur—nursing an attachment to a person twice my age who hasn't been "hip" for at least that long? After all, were I truly a well-adjusted individual, I would have forgotten my childish ties to Colts Neck, New Jersey (Exit 120 off the Garden State Parkway), in the whirlwind of college life. No reprimands for studying with Mötley Crüe inspiring my creative genius. No disembodied voice calling, "Don't you have an exam coming up?" just when I have sacked out in front of the TV with a bag of Doritos. Parties anywhere and any-time, with no one to answer to in the morning. Heck, I don't have to get up in the morning. . . .

Miss You "

Happily, with time and practice the homesickness and the sense of alienation became less acute; however, an equally odd state of affairs emerged in their place. I started to be disgusted by the mess around me. I dreamed of the day when I'd get the chance to hit the sack before midnight and looked forward to waking up to a sunrise instead of a sunset. The round-the-clock activity and partying that had riveted my attention now repulsed me with its glaring brilliance. I coveted the peace and solitude of my own dorm room with only an issue of *Sports Illustrated* to keep me company. I began to actually want to make my bed—every morning. In other words, I wanted all the things that my mother had always said I should but I said I never would—and I was liking it. . . .

College has given me friendships I wouldn't trade for anything—not even a slice of pizza on Broccoli Tofu Casserole night at the cafeteria. Here I have met people with whom I have deciphered mathematical hieroglyphics, conquered Mt. Häagen-Dazs in a single study break, and griped about the injustices or extolled the glories of the grading system (depending on my latest report card). This to me is true friendship—an intimate sharing of life's agonies and ecstasies and everything in between that renders a bond too precious to break.

My relationship with my mom—my confidante, my play-mate, my counselor—is one of these bonds. As such, it deserves every bit as much acknowledgement for its importance in my life as my college friendships do. My mom may not know the latest fashion trends, but she knows me better than anyone in the world. (Good thing too—I wouldn't want anybody else knowing all that stuff about me.) Somehow, when I'm with her now, I look forward to grocery shopping and picking up my dad's suits at the cleaners even when she doesn't take me to lunch "as long as we're out" or treat me to two frozen yogurts "just 'cause." I talk with her about life and politics and religion, not to make the best of being stuck in the car with her, but because she's an intelligent and thoughtful person. I discuss my sister's boyfriend problems and my dad's job stress-es and the neighbors' financial troubles, not just to gossip, but because she helps me understand, cope, and assist. I gripe about failed diets, phony friends, bad haircuts, and salespeople who make me buy clothes I don't want at a store I don't like with money I don't have. . . .

And despite popular opinion, I have come to accept that this—not my twenty-first birthday or staying up past David Letterman—is a sign of my maturity. The resemblance that people so often comment upon goes beyond a shared affinity for bagels or "the family nose"; I also share many of her values and beliefs, and they're reflected in the way I think, feel, and behave. Mom influenced this by raising me, but it was ultimately my decision to adopt some of her characteristics and teachings as my own. She is separate from me, yet she has helped make me what I am. . . .

—*Aimee Bingler*

I look at you and wonder,

When did this happen?

Where was I during your transformation

from scrawny kids,

to awkward teenagers,

to the grownups you've become?

We lost much, we three,

to the alcohol, its hold over me.

For that, I will ever feel a sense

of sadness, of regret.

And yet, seeing you now,

I am struck with a feeling of awe.

You have grown straight and true,

strong in character and self-sufficient.

I love you, and I'm so very proud

of both of you.

—Nancy D. Wall, Blackfoot, Idaho

Peggy Bair/St. Joseph News-Press, St. Joseph, Missouri

When my son came to live with us during a trial separation in his marriage, my motherly instincts immediately kicked in.

One day he said, "Mom, I love you, but I can take care of myself and fix my own meals. Don't worry about me."

It really hit me that no matter what happened to him (he soon was divorced), I would forever be a mom.

—Joanne Viner, San Diego, California

I marvel. Faint flutters of movement.

An intoxicating pink-lotioned head.

Teething and toddling. Five-year-old

frankness. Elementary antics, good

and bad. Junior high jitters. Osmotic

parental pain and insecurities. High

school headiness. Readiness?

Cars, late nights. I worry.

Dating, peer pressure, I worry.

Glimmers of independence.

The blink of an eye. Cap, gown, tassel.

The world beckons.

I let go.

—Mary Jedlicka Humston, Iowa City, Iowa

Letting go . . . it's what this job is all about, in the end. If I have nurtured, encouraged, directed, and supported you, my children,

then letting go should be a natural step. Trusting you to fly on your own is the best way I can show you my love.

—Yvonne Ohumukini-Urness, San Jose, California

Ron Nickel, Three Hills, Alberta

❧

I waited anxiously as three busloads of eighth-graders arrived home

after a week in New York City. Most of the parents viewed the trip

as an excellent opportunity for their child. But for me, it was a rehearsal.

I knew for certain that my little girl was going to embrace life with a passion—

and it was unlikely she would always live in Dublin, Ohio.

So it came as no surprise to me that after she disembarked the bus she ran to tell me,

"Mom, when I grow up I'm going to live in New York City!"

On the drive home, she recounted every exciting moment of her trip.

Then she asked what had happened at home while she was away.

I was delighted to be able to tell her the begonias had come into bloom.

She looked at me and smiled, and in an instant

I could see the not-so-distant future, to a time when a daughter

becomes a woman. When that time comes, I'll be meeting her plane, train, or bus

so that we can sit on the porch on a warm summer evening,

taking time to admire the blooming begonias.

—*Katanya Berndt, Dublin, Ohio*

K. C. Stephens, Shreveport, Louisiana

❧

I have been amazed that adolescence has been the best period in my daughters' lives. It is truly the culmination of childhood. If only I could keep them at this bright, funny, idealistic stage forever! But just as I become deeply aware of their perfection, and the little time we have left as a family unit, they activate all the independence skills we instilled in their youth. Isn't it ironic that we teach them to leave and then feel sad when they finally listen.

—*Kathryn Linhardt, Iowa City, Iowa*

❧

I knew there would come a day when I would have to cut the apron strings. But at fifteen and a half! I thought I was safe in consenting for you to be an exchange student because you had to be sixteen and your birthday was still months away. Surprise! Surprise! You were accepted!

—*Ethel Mae Spitler, Mesa, Arizona*

Marie Poirier Marzi, Gaithersburg, Maryland

My son left home today. And I remember this catch in my

throat—the same as when I watched his fat, five-year-old leg

strain to reach the top step of the school bus. That was a big

step for a little boy. Now, his battered, red Escort sputters

down the road, its front quarter-panel flapping.

Rust has eaten its body, but it has carried him faithfully

over many miles to our old hometown where

his childhood pals have become companions

of his young manhood.

He is going there, buoyant with optimism,

to share a rented house as humble as his car—

to conquer the world.

His horn squawks bravely, and I wave

for as long as I can see a red speck in the road.

—*Kate Convissor, Alto, Michigan*

When he leaves for college, my house is not empty. He still crawls across the rug, charming at one. Calls from his easel, Picasso at three.

Storms to his room in fury at eight. Builds spaceships at ten. Shows off his tux at sixteen. I house a crowd of children he's left behind.

After every departure I wonder: Did I hold him enough? Listen enough? Encourage enough? Love enough? Was I too busy? Impatient? Insistent?

It's not my empty nest that bothers me. It's living with the Ghosts of Children Past.

—*Patricia Sprinkle, Miami, Florida*

A MOTHER'S TOUCH

&

You cried solid for your first ten months. You should feel grateful your dad and I gave you four additional siblings.

Now as I watch you start out your new life with such joy and enthusiasm, those same exciting memories stir deep in my soul. I look in the mirror to see that girl in my past but instead

I see a mother who is going to cry solid for the next ten months.

—Dena Luthi, Freedom, Wyoming

&

I gave birth to the Velcro Baby.

We were joined at the hip from day one.

When Kessie was three and a half,

I asked her if she and I were the same

or if we were two different people.

She replied quite adamantly that we were the same.

That she was me and I, she.

Now, at five, she is just starting to separate.

When she turned five, however, she took

a giant leap backward in independence.

I recognized this as preparation for kindergarten,

a retreat and regroup maneuver.

So I gathered her in, hugged her a lot,

and told her she could stay with me all she wanted.

And in her own good time she was ready to venture forth.

I'll always be glad I took the time for her

when she needed me.

— Wendy Baylor Schmidt, Wilson, Wyoming

Nita Winter, Sausalito, California

LAUNCHER

I'll Love

Usually the moon shines bright on clear May nights in eastern Pennsylvania. But tonight the moon is missing. All is dark. I notice brown circles under the lamp in the hall when Mother welcomes our 2:00 A.M. arrival from Illinois. I also notice brown circles under her eyes. Spots I'd never noticed before. Tired skin under gentle folds.

But here she stands, my mother for forty years. I sense an accumulation of nights waiting up for home-coming children, as though the years have cast shadows from the lamp onto her face. I see the years in the black and blue veins that have just this week felt the heart specialist's probe. I hear the years—like the ocean ringing in a seashell—in the doctor's diagnosis. "Red flag . . . enlarged heart . . . slow the pace . . ." I stare into uncertainty. Mother has been a steady pulse through the years. Tomorrow has been an assumed promise—a grand procession of family weddings, births, graduations, music recitals, ordinations, Christmas, Easter, Thanksgiving. Time has been an event, not a sequence.

You Forever"

As I look at Mother, I sense that someone has wound the clock. Time now has a cadence. Years have become increments. History has a beginning and an end. I shiver in the early morning chill. But then Mother's arms wrap me in warmth, and I am home. A forty-year-old child reassured by her mother's touch. There is no time in touch. Welcoming arms know not the years.

I hear the tea kettle whistling. Freshly baked chocolate chip cookies wait on the old ironstone plate that once served cookies from Grandma Hollinger's kitchen. Mother's chocolate chip cookies and Grandma Hollinger's ironstone plate pull me back into timelessness. We sip peppermint tea and laugh over a silly story Daddy tells. Our laughter drowns out the clock. There is no time in laughter. Mother laughs the hardest of all. Dark circles. Tired circles of joy. Her children are home.

For a moment I forget bruised veins and ticking clocks. I am held together by things that do not change—a mother's early morning welcome, freshly baked chocolate chip cookies, an ironstone plate, peppermint tea, a mantel clock, and laughter. I am held together by a God who does not change. I know the God of time who is yet above time. I see tonight in my mother's face the strange paradox of time and timelessness. A rare glimpse of the divine.

—Ruth Senter

Angela Peterson, Orlando, Florida

&

I never wanted to be a mom. But then during

World War II, when my husband was called to

the service, I changed my mind.

From the moment of conception I knew that

my son would be perfect.

I wasn't disappointed.

—Venita E. Rex, San Jose, California

&

While growing up, the word *mom*

stirred in me many emotions—

love, hurt, confusion.

I had three moms, but as a teenager,

when I most needed a mom,

I had none.

For years I did not, would not,

call anyone "Mom." Then I met you,

the mother of my husband-to-be.

Now, I gladly use the word *mom*.

You have been everything to me

the word implies.

I love you, Mom!

—Pat Leeson, Vancouver, Washington

John Gilroy, Kalamazoo, Michigan

Mothers aren't supposed to outlive their children but I lost my daughter, Ginny. Cradled in my arms now is her beautiful

grandchild in whose eyes I catch a glimpse of my girl. *Your daughter is a good mother, Ginny. You'd be so proud of her.*

—*Virginia Triolo, Sparks, Nevada*

David Harrison, Topeka, Kansas

Tom Watson, Skaneateles Lake, New York

Being a mother is the highest calling for me!

—*Linetta Powell, Littleton, Colorado*

Thank you Mom, for your loving example,

which will continue to shine for generations

as my daughters become mothers and the cycle continues.

—*Monica Goering Cardiff, San Jose, California*

After my father died, Mother suffered several small strokes and came to live with my husband and me.

She never cried except late at night. Some of my dearest moments were holding her and rocking her while she cried out her loneliness.

—Gretchen Frederick, Middlebury, Indiana

As a volunteer mom cradling other mom's babies,

many with special challenges,

I reflect on my fifty-three years of marriage

and all the loving I've given to my own children

and my fourteen grandchildren.

You'd think I'd have run out of love by this time,

but I find I have more than enough to share.

—Katherine Bade, Ford, Washington

Nita Winter, Sausalito, California

I've been told that you can't really know love until you've had a child and lost it. I couldn't have children, though I tried everything possible.

When the doctors said I once may have had a miscarriage, I mourned even the thought. And two days after my divorce was final, I got a call from Social Services telling me that our baby

was waiting at the airport to be picked up. My ex-husband had said he would call the adoption agency to tell them our marriage had not survived, but he hadn't done it.

I had to tell the lady to give my baby to some other mom. So now I mourn two. I don't think my heart knows I didn't give birth to those two babies I lost.

—Nancy Lund, Sparks, Nevada

☙

I remember sitting by my mother's bed,

spooning pieces of grapefruit into her mouth.

I'd always imagined that when she and I reached this point

in our lives, I would lovingly take care of her with selfless joy.

Instead, I was angry that she was dying of emphysema

at age sixty-six and exhausted with the confusing

emotional struggles of role reversal.

I felt like a little girl still longing to be taken care of

by her mother—an adult, impatient that the aging

parent had become like a child.

As I stabbed at the grapefruit, I squirted myself in the eye

with some juice. "Oh!" I cried out, dropping the spoon.

And the tears of frustration came.

"I'm sorry," my mother whispered weakly,

and we both knew she wasn't

talking about the sting of the grapefruit juice.

—*Carol Kuykendall, Boulder, Colorado*

FOREVER MOTHER

☙

I've loved you, nurtured you, cared for you every waking moment.

You have brought so much laughter, love, and life into this family.

Our home has an emptiness with you gone, but in my heart, I hold you firmly, forever.

—*Sue Watson, Skaneateles Lake, New York*

It's the sense of family, getting together for special times, belonging, that makes being a mom so special.

It was all trial and error for me since my mom died when I was so young.

But it has been great being able to care for and help each of my children develop. There's always something that can be done for one of them.

And the most wonderful thing about motherhood is the love I receive in return.

—*Hanna Whitworth, San Diego, California*

Today I must say "Hello"

and "Goodbye" to my son,

Jacob. God determined

the days of his life.

It scared me to think

of delivering this child,

of naming him.

But if I, his mother,

could not, then who?

—*Dale Skram, Superior, Colorado*

Gus Chan, Cleveland Heights, Ohio

Bruce C. Strong, Orange, California

My child has died, lying on a bed in this cold room, hooked up to beeping monitors and whirring machines.

My world has changed with this birth and this death. I no longer look at my other children or anyone else's

in the same way. I want to grab these other women and shout at them, "Love that child, hold him while you

can. Because someday you may not be able to. And you will wish you had."

I only had him for six months. I thank God for each day of that time.

—*Angela Troiani, Bloomsburg, Pennsylvania*

A

Mo Latimer, San Diego, California

During one rather hectic, frustrating day with my infant daughter and my three-year-old son,

I began feeling sorry for myself and lamenting that I never have time to do anything

I want to do. Then it dawned on me that I was doing something I wanted to do.

I had wanted to be a mother! My artwork could wait until my babies were older.

Suddenly I had such a feeling of peace, and the stress vanished.

—*Victoria Laird, Oskaloosa, Iowa*

❧

Forty years have passed since my mother died, and I still miss her unconditional love.

—*Jane Keller, San Antonio, Texas*

❧

When my first child left home,

I felt the world had come to an end.

Little did I know I would feel the same

when the last two left.

My neighbor said, "They are like birds

and when they learn to fly

you must let them go."

So I did.

But I have always left

a little birdseed out,

and they fly back regularly.

I am truly blessed.

—*Beverly Cooke, Yorba Linda, California*

April Saul/Philadelphia Inquirer, Philadelphia, Pennsylvania

To My Child—

I hope someday you will know and

understand the love I feel for you

as I sign these adoption papers

allowing someone else to take you

and raise you as their own.

(You are so beautiful.)

My heart is breaking, but my soul

is rejoicing in this decision.

It's the right one.

(I'm only a child myself.)

I will miss you.

I will always love you.

I will cherish forever

this time together,

our time together,

as mother and daughter.

I love you,

Mom

—*An Anonymous Mom*

Anne Jorgensen/Photri Inc., Falls Church, Virginia

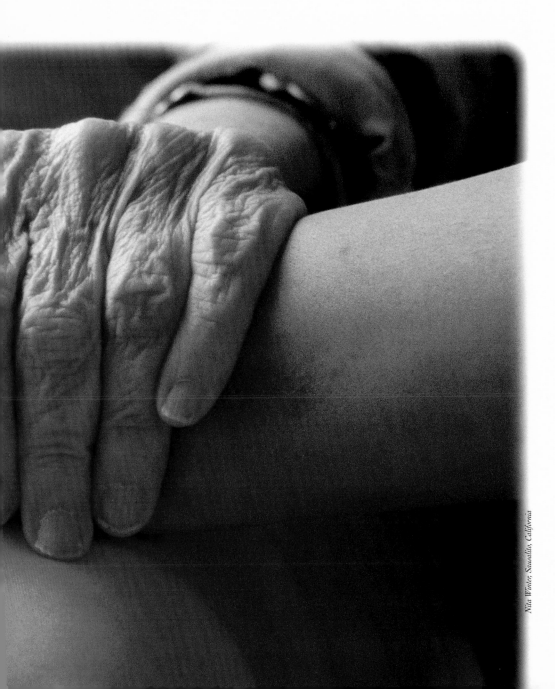

Nita Winter, Sausalito, California

Tucking the blankets

in around her frail body,

I lean over and softly kiss

the wrinkled cheek

of this sweet child

I call Mother.

Here, in the quiet of her room,

I sit recalling

the countless nights

she tucked me in,

kissed my forehead,

and whispered,

"Good night, Sweetheart."

—*Bertha Day, St. Johns, Arizona*

Credits

Tributes selected and edited by Elisa Morgan, Carol Kuykendall, and Mary Beth Lagerborg

All quotes by mothers are printed with permission and are not intended as photograph captions.

Berndt, Katanya. Excerpt reprinted from *Victoria*, May 1997. Copyright © 1997 by Katanya Berndt. Used in this abridged form with permission of the author.

Bingler, Aimee. "Mom-Sick." Excerpt reprinted from *Seventeen*, September 1991. Copyright © 1991 by Aimee Lynn Bingler. Used in this abridged form with permission of the author and *Seventeen*.

Bresnahan, Carla Risener. "My Mother's Lap." Excerpt reprinted from *Welcome Home*, May 1993. Mothers at Home, Inc., Vienna, Virginia (1-800-783-4666). Copyright © 1993 by Carla Risener Bresnahan. Used in this abridged form with permission of Carla Risener Bresnahan.

Brewer, Wendy C. "Today I Didn't Say the Right Things." Excerpt reprinted from *Decision*, May 1996. Copyright © 1996 by Wendy C. Brewer. Used with permission of the author.

Burton, Linda. "Unquality Time." Excerpt reprinted from *Discovering Motherhood*. Mothers at Home, Inc., Vienna, Virginia, 1991. Copyright © 1991 by Linda Burton. Used in this abridged form with permission of the author.

Campolo, Anthony. "A Dreamer for the Kingdom." Excerpt reprinted from *What My Parents Did Right*, edited by Gloria Gaither. Star Song Publishing Group/Jubilee Communications, Inc., Franklin, Tennessee, 1991. Copyright © 1991 by Matt Price. Used in this abridged form with permission of Matt Price. All rights reserved.

Carson, Ben. Excerpt reprinted from *Gifted Hands*. Copyright © 1990 by Review & Herald® Publishing Association. Used in the abridged form with permission of Zondervan Publishing House.

Clark, Sandra Bernlehr. "Can My Love Protect My Child?" Excerpt reprinted from *Today's Christian Woman*, May/June 1985. Copyright © 1985 by Sandra Bernlehr Clark. Used in this abridged form with permission of Sandra Bernlehr Clark.

Coogan, Jeanmarie. "My Mother Barked Like a Seal." Excerpt reprinted from *Reader's Digest*, May 1994, adapted from the original printed in *Ladies' Home Journal*, 1962. Copyright © 1962 by Meredith Corporation. Used with permission of *Reader's Digest*, *Ladies' Home Journal*, and Nell Coogan.

Fisher, Mary. Excerpt reprinted from *Sleep With The Angels, A Mother Challenges AIDS*. Moyer Bell, Wakefield, Rhode Island, 1994. Copyright © 1994 by Family AIDS Network. Used in this abridged form with permission of Moyer Bell.

Girard, Jennifer. Excerpt reprinted from *Letters to Our Daughters*. Beyond Words Publishing, Inc., Hillsboro, Oregon, 1997 (1-800-284-9673). Copyright © 1997 by Kristine Van Raden and Molly Davis. Used in this abridged form with permission of Jennifer Girard and Beyond Words Publishing.

Graham, Franklin. Excerpt reprinted from *Rebel With A Cause*. Thomas Nelson Publishers, Nashville, Tennessee. Copyright © 1995 by Thomas Nelson Publishers. Used with permission of the publisher.

Graham, Ruth Bell. Excerpt reprinted from *Prodigals and Those Who Love Them*. Focus on the Family Publishing, Colorado Springs, Colorado. Copyright © 1991 by Ruth Bell Graham. Used with permission of the author.

Huffman, Vicki. "Flight Clearance." Excerpt reprinted from *Today's Christian Woman*, September/October 1986. Copyright © 1986 by Vicki Huffman. Used in this abridged form with permission of Vicki Huffman.

Jackson, Marni. Excerpt reprinted from *The Mother Zone: Love, Sex, and Laundry in the Modern Family*. Henry Holt and Company, Inc., New York, New York, 1992. Copyright © 1992 by Marni Jackson. Used in this abridged form with permission of Henry Holt and Company, Inc.

L'Engle, Madeleine. Reprinted from *Mothers & Daughters*. Harold Shaw Publishers, Wheaton, Illinois, 1997. Copyright © 1997 by Crosswicks, Ltd. Used with permission of Harold Shaw Publishers.

Lott, Juanita Tamayo. "The Making of a Mother." Reprinted from *Discovering Motherhood*. Mothers at Home, Inc., Vienna, Virginia, 1991. Copyright © by Juanita Tamayo Lott. Used in this abridged form with permission of Juanita Tamayo Lott.

McGinnis, Eva. "Abundance." Reprinted from *Welcome Home*, vol. 14, no. 9, September 1997. Mothers at Home, Inc., Vienna, Virginia. Copyright © 1997 by Eva McGinnis. Used with permission of Eva McGinnis.

Moore, Gerald. "The Day Mom Cried." Excerpt reprinted from *Reader's Digest*, September 1980. Copyright © 1980 by The Reader's Digest Association, Inc. Used with permission of *Reader's Digest*.

Quindlen, Anna. Excerpt reprinted from *Living Out Loud*. Copyright © 1988 by Anna Quindlen. Used with permission of Random House, Inc., under "fair usage."

Rockwell, Susan. "Kitchen Dancing." Excerpt reprinted from *Welcome Home*, March 1991. Mothers at Home, Inc., Vienna, Virginia. Copyright © by Susan Rockwell. Used with permission of the author.

Senter, Ruth. "When the Moon Doesn't Shine." Excerpt reprinted from *Surrounded by Mystery*. Zondervan Publishing House, Grand Rapids, Michigan, 1988. Copyright © 1988 by Ruth Senter. Used with permission of the author.

Tchividjian, Gigi Graham. Excerpt reprinted from *Currents of the Heart*. Multnomah Books, Inc., Sisters, Oregon. Copyright © 1996 by Gigi Graham Tchividjian. Used in this abridged form with permission of Multnomah Books.

Wangerin, Jr., Walter. "How Precious Did That Grace Appear." Excerpt reprinted from *Little Lamb, Who Made Thee?* Zondervan Publishing House, Grand Rapids, Michigan, 1994. Copyright © 1993 by Walter Wangerin, Jr. Used in this abridged form with permission of Zondervan Publishing House.

West, Marion Bond. "Mama's Plan." Reprinted from *Guideposts* magazine. Copyright © 1988 by Guideposts, Carmel, New York. Used with permission of Guideposts.

Wilkins, Deborah Potter. "Full Circle." First printed in *Welcome Home*, December 1997. Mothers at Home, Inc. Vienna, Virginia. Copyright ©1997 by Deborah Potter Wilkins. Used by permission of the author.

Yates, Susan Alexander and Allison Yates Gaskins (editors). "You Stood By Me." Excerpt reprinted from *Thanks, Mom, for Everything*. Servant Publications, Ann Arbor, Michigan, 1997. Copyright © 1997 by Susan Alexander Yates and Allison Yates Gaskins. Used in this abridged form with permission of Servant Publications.

Youngs, Bettie B. "The Little Glass Chip." Excerpt reprinted from *Values From the Heartland*. Health Communications, Inc., Deerfield Beach, Florida, 1995. Copyright © 1995 by Bettie B. Youngs. Used in this abridged form with permission of Health Communications, Inc.

Original floral watercolor illustrations by Thomas G. Lewis

MOPS International

MOPS (Mothers of Preschoolers) is a program designed to encourage mothers with children under school age. As a ministry of a local church, MOPS provides a caring, accepting atmosphere for today's mothers of preschoolers. Contact MOPS International to see if there is a MOPS group near you: 303-733-5353 or 800-929-1287.
E-mail: Info@mops.org. Internet: www.mops.org.

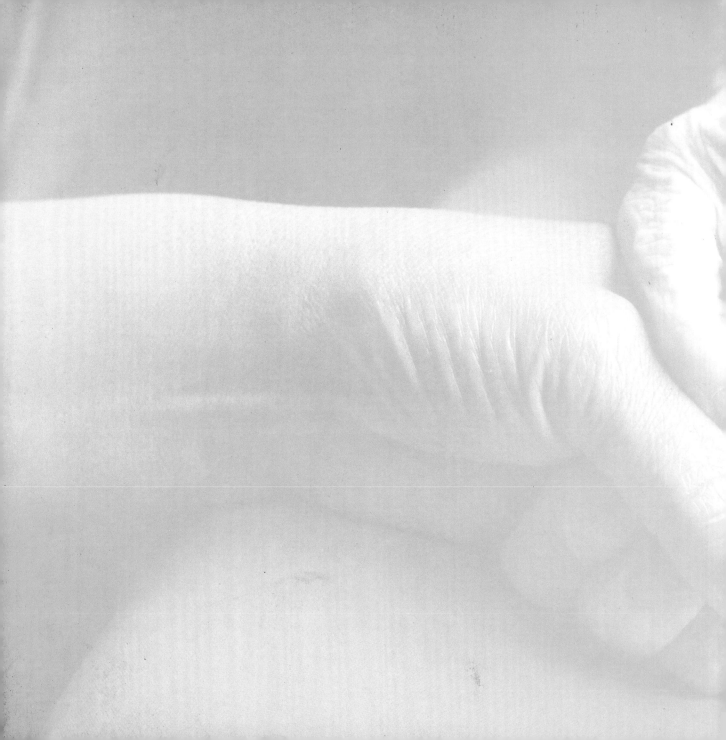